16.95

THROUGH
THESE
PORTALS

From Immigrant to
University President

By Rolf A. Weil, President Emeritus, Roosevelt University

Library of Congress Cataloging-in-Publication Data

Through These Portals: From Immigrant to University President

By Rolf A. Weil

1. Biography. 2. History. 3. Roosevelt University. 4. Rolf A. Weil

This Volume Is Dedicated
To My Wife Leni
Whose Support And Love Was
The Essential Ingredient For Success

Table of Contents

ACKNOWLEDGMENTS

I retired from the presidency of Roosevelt University in August of 1988 after 42 years of teaching and administration. My successor, Dr. Theodore Gross, suggested that it might be useful to record my reflections on the history of Roosevelt University. He kindly read key chapters of the manuscript and made helpful suggestions.

I wish to express my deep gratitude to members of the "Roosevelt University family" for underwriting this publication. John Joseph, Vice President for Development, and Connie Zonka, Director of Public Relations, were instrumental in bringing this venture to fruition.

Dr. Dominic Martia read the entire manuscript and made editorial as well as substantive recommendations from the vantage point of an English professor, a former Roosevelt University student, and a current vice president. I am most grateful for his friendship.

Jerome Stone not only has been kind enough to write a preface to this volume but has been a major source of moral and financial support during our 15 year partnership between an exemplary board chairman and a university president.

Mary Sonoda, who has been associated with the President's office since 1945 and has worked continuously at Roosevelt University for over four decades, typed the manuscript, gathered information and provided invaluable assistance.

Finally, I want to thank students, alumni, faculty members, administrators, trustees, and friends of Roosevelt University who contributed so much not only to my career but to the enlightenment of our society. Particular mention should be made of my early mentors, the late Professor Walter Weisskopf, economist and social scientist, and Dr. Otto Wirth, scholar and humanist.

I

Roosevelt University Chronology

1945   April   *Franklin D. Roosevelt dies.*

Charter for Roosevelt College issued.

Edward J. Sparling named President of Roosevelt College and Edwin R. Embree of Rosenwald Fund named Chairman of the Board.

Sept.   *Over 1,300 students enrolled in building at 231 South Wells Street.*

Nov.   *Mrs. Eleanor Roosevelt dedicated new College in memory of her husband "...to the enlightenment of the human spirit through the constant search for truth, and to the growth of the human spirit through knowledge, understanding and good-will."*

1946   *Roosevelt College receives full accreditation.*

Roosevelt purchases Sullivan and Adler designed Auditorium Building.

1947   *Roosevelt moves to Auditorium Building.*

1948   *Harold Ickes, long-time U.S. Secretary of the Interior, elected Chairman of the Board after death of Embree.*

1949   *Enrollment reaches 6,000 students.*

1950   *Leo Lerner becomes third Board Chairman.*

1951   *Graduate Division established.*

1954   *Roosevelt College becomes Roosevelt University.*

Chicago Musical College, founded in 1867 by Florenz Ziegfeld, becomes part of Roosevelt University and its president, Rudolph Ganz, joins Roosevelt University faculty.

1955   *Special convocation to award honorary degrees to Eleanor Roosevelt, Earl Warren, and Dr. Jonas Salk.*

Extension courses established.

1959   University rededicated in the name of Eleanor as well as Franklin Delano Roosevelt.

Harland H. Allan becomes Board Chairman.

1962   Division of Continuing Education and Extension established to meet needs of adult and non-traditional students.

Favor-Ruhl Building on Wabash Avenue acquired as future site for student union and dormitory.

1963   Edward J. Sparling retires.

Lyle M. Spencer, President of Science Research Associates, elected Board Chairman.

Robert J. Pitchell appointed President.

1964   Rolf A. Weil appointed Acting President.

1966   Peace Corps Training Program for Sierra Leone initiated.

1967   Reopening of Auditorium Theatre.

Rolf A. Weil inaugurated as President in Auditorium Theatre.

1968   Chicago Musical College celebrates 100th Anniversary.

1969   Jerome Stone, CEO of Stone Container Corporation, elected Chairman of Roosevelt University Board, a position he held for 15 years.

1970   Twenty-fifth anniversary celebrated.

$2 million gift from the Heller Foundation leading to building of Heller Center, naming of School of Business Administration and establishing Heller Lectures on International Business.

College of Continuing Education, later renamed the Evelyn T. Stone University College is established.

1971   Herman Crown Center Student Union Dormitory is dedicated.

University Tower remodeled with the help of government funds.

1972   Auditorium Building lobby restored with the support of Edgar Kaufman and architect John Vinci.

College of Education established.

1973 *O'Malley Theater dedicated.*

1975 *Auditorium Building named national historic landmark.*

1978 *Arlington Heights campus established and later named the Albert A. Robin Campus.*

1980 *Expansion of Journalism Program.*

1981 *Ganz Hall renovation .*

1982 *Roosevelt University featured nationally on CBS in commentary by Dan Rather.*

1983 *Bart van Eck succeeds Jerome Stone as Board Chairman.*

1984 *Hospitality Management Program, later named for Manfred Steinfeld, inaugurated.*

Norman and Freda Mesirow Chair in Music established.

Eleanor Roosevelt Centennial Celebration.

1985 *College of Continuing Education (University College) named for Evelyn T. Stone (Mrs. Jerome H. Stone).*

1986 *Formal naming of Arlington Heights Campus for Albert E. Robin.*

Alan Anixter succeeds Bart van Eck as Chairman.

1987 *Seymour Logan Chair in History established.*

Arthur Rubloff bequest of $3 million announced.

Marvin Moss bequest of about $3 million for new facilities announced.

President Weil announced his retirement at end of '88 fiscal year after 23 years as President.

1988 *Dr. Theodore Gross was appointed President of Roosevelt University effective with Rolf A. Weil's retirement after 23 years at end of August.*

Twenty-five million dollar Landmark of Quality Campaign completed.

Harold Washington Chair established.

PREFACE

I first met Rolf Weil (although I didn't know this until years later) at a country club on the south side of Chicago. I was out there to play golf, while Rolf Weil was a young immigrant with gainful employment, he was shining shoes. It was only later, as a Board member of Roosevelt University in the early 1950's that I met Rolf, then the Dean of the Business College, and since that time we have had a lively and constructive association built around our common interests at Roosevelt University, and in solid friendship in many other activities around Chicago.

Rolf's Title, "From Immigrant to University President," reminds me of a passage in John W. Gardner's book, *Excellence.* When he points out, "The man who struggles from lowly beginnings to the top of the heap is fiercely motivated. Similarly, when a group forces its way to the top, a group of pioneers—or immigrants—their most precious asset is their drive, their sense of purpose, their indomitability. (They have) the will to win, the fierce determination born of struggle."

Rolf Weil traces the early life of an upper middle class family in Germany, whose world fell apart when the Nazis rose to power. He could have been discouraged, as Housman quoted, "I, a stranger alone and afraid, in a world I never made". He does portray graphically the struggle to begin life anew in America, learning different customs, a new language, and American work habits. This he did, with brilliance and courage. And thus, his story really unfolds as he begins his first teaching position at Roosevelt College.

This "upstart" college started in 1945, which was a pretty special year; World War II had ended, the atomic bomb had been revealed. Hitler committed suicide, Churchill was defeated. The year 1945 was the start of the Berlin problem, it marked the beginning of the population explosion.

Some say it was the first *American* year. Until then, America exercised enormous influence and was a prime mover in world affairs, but in 1945 we became the country the rest of the world reacted to and against. It was the year that Franklin Delano Roosevelt died, and later that same year, those of us involved with the school will never forget, Eleanor Roosevelt made a moving and prophetic speech in conjunction with the dedication of the University. She pointed out that, "The war has changed the whole world, and from now on we who talked about democracy have got to live it, because we must prove by our example to the world that democracy is not just a word, but something that through education you can achieve." She then dedicated Roosevelt College to "The enlightenment of the human spirit".

• • • • •

The founding of Roosevelt University was indeed a daring achievement, without precedent in the history of higher education. Rolf Weil has written movingly about Roosevelt's unique role as a school whose only standards were to admit students on academic merit alone, without quotas or prejudice to any minority.

Few universities were born into such unpromising circumstances. When it was chartered in May of 1945, the University had no campus, no library, no laboratory equipment and worse yet—no money or endowment funds. But its founders believed in an ideal which was far ahead of its time.

These courageous men and women were determined to create a university in Chicago where intelligent, industrious students—regardless of their race, creed or color—could have the opportunity to progress to the limits of their abilities. Years later this concept of "upward mobility" within a democratic framework became a governing principle of higher education. But in 1945, it was a bold assertion of faith.

Throughout its history, these qualities of determination and enterprise have continued to characterize Roosevelt. Roosevelt University has always been free to pioneer new academic concepts and innovative programs that would be difficult, if not impossible, for public institutions to attempt. The uniqueness of Roosevelt University is evident in its organization, its curriculum, its concern for students and its versatile faculty.

From a humble beginning, Roosevelt has grown to be one of this country's outstanding urban universities. Many of the radical concepts and innovations which Roosevelt pioneered more than 45 years ago are widely accepted today. An indication of the impact Roosevelt University has had on higher education is how more than 40,000 students have received their degrees from the University. It is the *only* non-sectarian private university serving primarily the Chicago area.

Rolf Weil sketches on a broad canvas the accomplishments of many of the men and women associated with the college and later the University—that made it all possible. Looking back on 45 years, we must never forget the effort and performance, the wisdom and courage of their leaders. They must cherish what Alfred North Whitehead called, "The habitual vision of greatness".

Certainly one of those with that kind of vision was Rolf Weil. At the retirement party that he mentions in the book, I jokingly referred to an outline of specifications for a university president that was a compendium of material information picked up by some others and added to by me. Thus, I pointed out that one search committee had used the following qualifications:

1. The President should have the charisma of a Franklin Roosevelt, John Kennedy or Dwight Eisenhower.

2. He should have demonstrated capacity for leadership.

3. He should be an educational statesman with excellent concepts for the development of the University.

4. He should be able to convince the students, the faculty, the trustees, the American Association of University Professors, the Association of Governing Boards and the friends of the college of the value of his concepts and enlist everybody's enthusiastic and unanimous support.

5. He must be popular with the students. He must also be a strict disciplinarian, forbidding drinking, gambling, etc. and other frivolous conduct among the students.

6. He must be a recognized scholar, hopefully having achieved the Nobel Prize, or its equivalent.

7. A prospective president must be a good fund-raiser. He should be able to raise all the money needed himself, and not call upon the trustees and other persons for help.

8. He should have an exemplary married and family life; hopefully married to a person related to the Rockefellers, Vanderbilts, Astors or the Fords.

9. He should be a good religious person, but if all of the attributes from 1 through 8 are handled equitably, then number 9 is not as much of a consequence.

Seriously, the President does fulfill multiple roles. He is the executive officer to our Board. He helps the Board define its place in the academic community and helps us to occupy that place. He is presiding officer of the faculty and as such he must assist the faculty senate in arriving at decisions and recommendations affecting the purposes, programs and behavior of the institution. He is administrator and chief of the support services that enable the University to operate and to perform its vital output of instruction, research, public service and constructive social criticism.

And the President, of necessity, is invested with the techniques of leadership, planning, budgeting, community affairs, personnel and reporting.

Thus, our University President encounters difficulties of multiple accountability even as he fulfills the multiple roles of the presidency. Just as universities comprise a unique enterprise, part of a unique social institution, so the college or university president has unique roles to master. He confronts never-ending challenges, but the president also must and should discover substantial satisfactions as well.

This, Rolf Weil did with distinction, courage and energy. Both he and his wife, Leni, threw themselves into the activities of the School to such an extent that Dan Rather, as a commencement speaker, became so impressed with the school and its graduates that he did an in-depth study and later broadcast in his nationwide commentator's role:

"Roosevelt isn't an old school. It was founded in

1945, the month Franklin D. Roosevelt died. The president is Rolf Weil, who fled Germany in the 30's and put himself through The University of Chicago. He wound up teaching at Roosevelt and didn't want to leave.

"Neither did his wife, Leni, who also fled Germany in the 30's and is one of Roosevelt's chief supporters. The Weils helped make Roosevelt what it is today."

Rolf traces several periods of crisis in his 23 years of administration. Certainly one of the most dramatic was that period of the sixties when open revolt from the students was the norm. As a matter of fact, when I was elected Chairman of the Board in 1968, I received a telegram of congratulations from my daughter, then a Junior at the University of Wisconsin, signed "Comrade Cynthia." Humorous or not, these were dangerous years for the universities and those whose leadership lacked courage and foresight suffered. Roosevelt was fortunate to have Rolf Weil at the helm. He did not run to the Board asking for guidance. Instead, he mapped out a program that was constructive to all students and appreciated by the majority. It was firm and fair, and the University's administration never lost control. I have often told Rolf that he could have been President of a major international corporation in the way he handled the many crises during those truculent years.

Thus, Roosevelt in its first 45 years has never had the seclusion or romantic ivy-covered vision of what many American colleges represented. Just as in the 60's, when the tensions, conflicts and outbursts of bad blood reflected society as a whole, we are now, in 1991, seeing another public crisis on campus. We have talk of political correctness, of universities doing "creative accounting" on Federal research grants, of anti-trust violations at Ivy League Schools, and of the questioning of standards used by agencies that accredit colleges and universities.

And thus, what looked like the first great disturbance of the status quo of university life in the 1960's has emerged as a lack of confidence on the public's part over the university's basic role. This began with the attack by former Secretary of Education William J. Bennett on those universities teaching what he called "faddish courses", was echoed by Professor Allan Bloom of the University of Chicago whose book. "The Closing of the American Mind," detailed concern over what we call higher education, and now can be seen as the Congress requires colleges and universities to evaluate and report on campus crime, athletic subsidies and research costs.

This state of unrest calls for leadership that will capture the sense of mission encompassed by the need for higher education. These leaders must have the capacity and vision to lead, and they must have followers who share their vision. A man like Rolf Weil is a model whose devotion to an ideal, and the courage to follow it through, defines the function of higher education to be the best it can be.

This book mirrors our own democratic values. The author shows as he looks back on his life, one molded in the crucible of hardship, of migrating to this country with nothing but individual and moral values, that by dint of hard and unremitting work and courage and sacrifice, one can emerge into the sunlit spaces of achievement, contentment and happiness.

Anais Nin once wrote in her diary that "an individual has the gift for elevating incident into destiny".

We are fortunate that Rolf Weil did come to our American shores. We are privileged that, in his retirement years he has given us this chronology of events at Roosevelt University in this rewarding book. He has chronicled not only his own life, but has paid tribute to others who made Roosevelt a great urban university. The school, and those who made it possible serves as a fine symbol of what makes America a truly great society.

Jerome H. Stone
Chairman Emeritus
Board of Trustees
Roosevelt University

INTRODUCTION

This small volume. although biographical, is not an auto-biography. While my life has spanned one of the most eventful and disturbing periods in the history of mankind, I do not intend to bore readers with personal details. Rather, I wish to record some of the thoughts, sentiments and theories that have evolved from my experience as a German immigrant who became bicultural over a long period of years. Much of this volume also offers a subjective view of the history of Roosevelt University, where I spent over four decades of my career.

My life began during the hyperinflation of 1920's Germany. Memories of a happy childhood in the later '20s and early '30s dimmed as I experienced the upheaval created by the rape of German democracy, the evils of national socialism, the Nazi persecution of the Jews, the flight to freedom in America, and the difficult task of cultural and economic integration into American society. My adjustment from the structured humanistic education in a German gymnasium in Stuttgart to the cafeteria-style liberal American high school education undoubtedly led to education at all levels becoming my major interest in life. Starting with a wonderful undergraduate experience in the College of the University of Chicago during Robert Maynard Hutchins' term, I benefited from the superb professional education provided by the university's academic economists. This led to my economic research and civil service work in the mid 1940s after the war. My career has paralleled the history of Roosevelt University (original-ly Roosevelt College). At this unique institution, dedicated to the concept of equal educational opportunity for all, I have had rich teaching and administrative experience culminating in a twenty-three year term as president from 1965 to 1988.

My commitment to education as a primary means for self-fulfillment has been total. While I do not share in the commonly held American belief that education makes for "goodness" and democracy, I do firmly believe that education is the most effective way of investing in human capital, thereby paying dividends in the form of upward mobility opportunities which contribute to socio-political stability. However, American education is facing a great crisis, particularly in urban areas. Its loss of rigor and standards will seriously affect America's global role for generations. Our nation's treasured values, democracy and freedom are going to be increasingly jeopardized if, through a lowering of standards for both students and faculty, excessive freedom and licentiousness, and a flight from the liberal arts, we lose a striving for excellence, a dedication to institutional responsibility and self-discipline essential for greatness.

During my career I have witnessed a shift from an emphasis on education as an end in itself and as a general preparation for life to an ever narrower professionalized and specialized system. I have seen a decline in the dedication of the teaching profession to its mission and a concomitant shift towards "bread and butter" objectives exemplified by increasing unionization of academicians and the growth of credentializing guilds disguised as professional accrediting agencies. These trends compel me to convey my thoughts about American higher education during the last four decades from my unique vantage point. Roosevelt University, which I have served for 42 years as a faculty member, department chairman, dean, and president, is an urban, heterogeneous, non-sectarian, commuter institution which has been a training ground for people of all ages, races and ethnic origins who have served this nation in scholarly pursuits, in business, in the arts, and as teachers. This institution began on a shoestring and with an idealism not only in terms of non-discrimination but also with great dedication to faculty participation in governance. I doubt if any other university has ever had seven elected faculty members on the Board, votes of confidence every three years for deans and the president and full participation by three elected faculty members in budget making. There is much to say about the advantages and pitfalls of such governance.

Finally, I must confess up front that some of my thoughts and values result from my immigrant roots and German upbringing. I owe much to American generosity—it is possible that only in this country could a poor refugee member of a minority religion have a career culminating in a university presidency. My friend and colleague, Dr. Otto Wirth, was fond of quoting Goethe: "Der Mensch kann nicht über senen eigenen Schatten springen" or "man cannot jump over his own shadow." Clearly, my views are influenced by my early and rather cosmopolitan origin.

Part I.

Portals to Freedom

"The truth is found

when men are

free to pursue it."

Franklin Delano Roosevelt, President of the United States
and Roosevelt University Namesake, 1882-1945

Education in Stuttgart
1928 to 1936

Although I was born in Pforzheim, we relocated to Stuttgart when I was four years old because my father was transferred there by the Singer Sewing Machine Company. My parental ancestry traces back for many generations to the Freiberg area and my maternal grandparents, the landowners, lived in Nürtingen on the Neckar River. My elementary school years were happy ones at Falkert-Schule in Stuttgart. We spent many weekends and vacations in Nürtingen, which in the '20s was still fairly rural. Little did I realize how those early years of great political ferment and frustrations resulting in the Nazi upheaval would greatly change our lives.

Although Jewish by religion, my family was ecumenical in its outlook. Considering later shocks, perhaps we were too nationalistic. I grew up hearing a great deal about the military experiences of my grandfather and father, who retold of their respective experiences in the Franco-Prussian War of 1970-71 and World War I, when my father served in the 126th and 248th regiments of Württemberg.

My early education was German to the core, both at home and in school. Although I am not a Freudian psychologist, I believe that my formative years not only developed my value system but influenced my attitudes toward educational issues and public policy in general.

I have been visually handicapped since the first year of my life. I am extremely grateful both to my parents and the German school system for having emphasized that with extra effort there was practically nothing I should be unable to do even with the corrected vision of only 20/100. Indeed, I frequently think that much harm is done by those educators who excessively pamper people with particular handicaps by putting them into specialized classrooms. Not that I mean to denigrate the need for special education, but I believe it is important for people to adjust on their own as much as possible. I became a fast reader mainly because I learned to recognize the shapes of words rather than individual letters. No one taught me this technique, but it has helped me tremendously throughout my career.

As was customary in Germany at the time, fateful educational decisions were made when children finished their fourth year of school. My parents wanted me to pursue a pre-academic course of study, which resulted in my taking the Aufnahmeprüfung examination for the Eberhard-Ludwigs Gymnasium, which consisted of a written test administered in the morning and composed of three parts—dictation, composition and arithmetic. The dictation portion was designed to test spelling and punctuation. The composition portion required a choice of one of three topics and tested one's ability to organize material and to write with style and imagination. In the arithmetic section one not only needed the skills of manipulating numbers, including fractions and decimals, but also to use shortcuts and logic in the interpretation of "story" problems. In the afternoon, we returned to the examination room to hear the list of students who were excused from taking the oral examination. The minutes that it took to get from "A" to "W" in the reading of these names seemed endless. After hearing my name listed as one of those who could go home, I still remember that afternoon as one of the happiest times in my childhood. I also remember my family's pride in what was, with hindsight, a small accomplishment.

The German system of making major educational decisions at such an early age has often been criticized and with some justification. Fortunately, the system has been modified so that today there is much greater flexibility and "late bloomers" are enabled in the various German Länder (states) to transfer more easily at later stages.

What remains highly controversial is the educational policy of classifying children by ability levels, not only through the type of "tracking" frequently used in American schools, but by physical separation and by major curriculum differences. There is no doubt that teaching in the German system is easier because this ability grouping stimulates learning and creates pride. However, such a system also tends toward a certain degree of elitism. For example, the Eberhard-Ludwigs Gymnasium which I attended was located right next to the old Hoppenlau Cemetery in which Uhland, Möricke and Hauff lay buried. Our teachers would frequently admonish us to live up to the traditions set by these great men. Indeed, at moments of our revealed incompetence, the teachers would tell us that these great Swabian poets and thinkers were "turning over in their graves" because of our ignorance.

The experiences of Jewish children in the German school system varied greatly from school to school and from city to city. Except for a rare remark about my ancestors "having killed Christ," I did not suffer from any overt anti-Semitism before I dropped out of the Gymnasium late in 1936 because of our impending emigration. Of course, after January of 1933, life in school became more difficult for both Jewish students and those reasonable teachers who were not in total sympathy with the new regime. The rector of the E-L Gymnasium, Dr. Binder, in fact, objected in 1933 to the flying of the Swastika, but he soon was given no choice in this matter. It was amazing to me, however, to see some teachers in 1933 already appearing in Nazi uniform at special school occasions.

At the Gymnasium there were two classrooms for each grade level. One classroom was made up of only Protestants, explained by the fact that Stuttgart was a predominantly Protestant city. The other room had Protestants, Catholics and three Jewish students out of a group of about thirty. Religious instruction was part of the educational requirement. The Protestant students were taught by the "homeroom" (Klassenlehrer) teacher and Catholic students were visited by a priest. But Jewish students at the lower grade levels had to attend a Jewish school next to the synagogue on Wednesday afternoons. As a result, I had a "free" period when others were getting Christian instruction. The "homeroom" teacher invited me to participate in the Protestant religious instructions if I so desired. I certainly preferred that invitation to walking around in the courtyard. To this day, I am amused that my grade in Christian instruction was considerably better than that obtained from the Jewish school. The perfectly reasonable decision by the classroom teacher to average the two grades was a frequent subject of conversation at our house.

Gradually, during the years 1933-1936, more and more of my classmates joined the Hitler Jugend. I am convinced that most of these young classmates, at least initially, had no political ideology and came from homes that had no enthusiasm for national socialism. In fact, I must admit that in a childish way I was subconsciously jealous of their ability to participate in enjoyable activities. My best friend at the Gymnasium was Helmut Bäuerle, whose father Theodor was a prominent educator who became, after the war, Kultusminister of Württemberg-Baden. The Bäuerle family were staunch democrats and did not have an anti-Semitic bone in their bodies. I spent a lot of my free time at their home and in the winter of 1935-36 they were even willing to take the risk of inviting me to go skiing with them. Helmut joined the Hitler youth movement and on special occasions had to wear his uniform to school. On one such day my father picked me up at school by automobile and a group of my uniformed friends jumped into the car with me. My father was greatly embarrassed and admonished me never to invite anyone in uniform again because of possible adverse consequences for them and for us.

One of the Nazis' educational innovations was the establishment of Landschulheime (country school camps), which provided an opportunity for physical education and political indoctrination. The two other Jewish students in my class and myself were not allowed to participate and were sent to the Karlsgymnasium in another part of the city. There I suffered discrimination and abuse and was looked upon as an unwanted intruder.

One of the most shocking and humiliating experiences of my youth occurred when my class went to the public swimming pool and I discovered that a sign had been posted prohibiting

Jews from swimming there. In my later years as an administrator at Roosevelt University, I often resented the comments from some black students that as a white man I could not understand their history of discrimination. To me, of course, my experience felt even more humiliating since I had previously enjoyed an environment of equality.

During 1933 and 1934 my parents never dreamed of leaving the land of their birth. My aunt kept saying "Just let Hitler try to run the government and he will fail very soon." She was obviously mistaken and emigration became a consideration when it became increasingly clear that Hitler was going to remain in power and that the discrimination supported by radical laws was going to become increasingly severe.

One of the most demonic techniques of the Nazi government was how it divided the Jewish community in the early years. Distinctions were made which provided somewhat greater security for families such as ours where the head of the household had served in the front lines during the first World War. My father had been active in the Jewish war veterans organization (Reichsbund Jüdischer Frontsoldaten) and in the early years of the Nazi period we were convinced that we would continue to get preferential treatment—that we could wait until this ugly period in German history "blew over". How gullible we and many other German Jews were to believe that past service to our government would reap rewards. Many later paid with their lives for their faith in the old imperial phrase of World War I: "Der Dank des Vaterlands Ist euch gewiss" (The gratitude of the fatherland is assured).

In 1935, however, my parents thought it might be a good precaution to send me to a boarding school in Switzerland and in the summer I ended up at Lausanne. The main purpose for this was so I could acquire enough fluency in French in order to later attend the Ecole de Commerce on a more permanent basis. I returned to Germany at the end of the summer. My Swiss educational experience came to an abrupt end because my parents had concluded that we would have to emigrate. This fact became obvious (fortunately, in hindsight) because of the reaction of my father's company to an article in the Stuttgart Nazi newspaper, *Das Flammenzeichen,* which attacked the American-owned subsidiary for being foreign and for employing a Jew in a leading executive position. Singer was not going to risk losing its profitable German operation and it was clear that my father would either have to find another position in Germany or leave the country. Singer offered him positions in Hungary, Turkey or Jaffa in Palestine. My father wisely rejected Budapest, had no stomach for moving to Ankara and explored the Jaffa possibility in the spring of 1936, when Arab-Jewish disturbances were occurring in this all-Arab city. My father felt this would be an inappropriate move. So he returned to Stuttgart and we made plans to emigrate to the United States without any employment assurances and the knowledge that U.S. economic conditions were then abominable.

Getting a visa to go to the United States was not easy in the 1930s. Although the German quota, under the "National Origins" Law, was not filled until after the Kristalnacht of 1938, the American consulates in Germany seemed intentionally slow in processing applications. There is considerable evidence that American State Department anti-Semitism played some role in these delays. To get a visa one needed an affidavit of support from a U.S. citizen. Fortunately, two of my grandfather's brothers had emigrated in the late nineteenth century and were in a financial position to grant affidavits. However, fearful of having to support the new immigrants, they provided the affidavit only for my father, with the understanding that after he was "settled," they would send for us. This was, obviously, a very tense period in our lives—the delays and corruption at the American Consulate did not make things easier. The consulate secretary at the time was the notorious Mr. Fuchs, whose paper-shuffling powers and number-assigning responsibilities enabled him to extort bribes from desperate refugees.

My father left for the United States in August of 1936 and my mother and I were able to follow in December. During this waiting period we had a dreadful experience. As we prepared to emigrate we knew we could not take more than an insignificant amount of money out of the country. My mother decided to have some of our massive German furniture modernized and reduced in size and she arranged with a cabinetmaker for this work at a pre-arranged price. When the furniture was delivered, this craftsman asked for twice that amount. My mother said she would not pay it and he left in anger, only to return a few hours later with two storm-troopers. My mother, understandably but foolishly, tried to remind this fellow of the anti-Nazi sentiments he had expressed to her weeks earlier. This dispute could only lead to trouble, so I cut off my mother's conversation and persuaded her to pay the exorbitant amount rather than risk a confrontation with the uniformed Nazis.

When it became my mother's and my turn to apply for our visas, another nerve-wracking experience awaited us. The American Consulate invested in physical examinations for all visa applicants. Many people were turned down for such reasons as heart disease, diabetes, etc. My performance in reading the eye chart was not satisfactory and I was sent to a consulting ophthalmologist. My visa was issued but with an attached and sealed envelope to be opened by immigration officials in New York harbor. Obviously, the fear of being sent back made the ocean crossing a psychological nightmare. Fortunately, we landed in New York at Christmas without further difficulty, with 40 marks (or $10) each in our pockets and a Leica around each of our necks. The Leicas brought $50 apiece, which was enough to live on for about a month. We were met at the pier by a childhood friend of my mother's from Nürtingen. Late that evening we stopped off at a New York drug store ice cream fountain, the type of retail establishment totally unknown in Germany at the time. My first taste of America was a chocolate soda. That pleasant pause was cruelly disturbed by the news that we had to rush to Chicago because my father, in order to await our arrival, had delayed emergency surgery for a hyperthyroid condition. On December 31 we arrived at Chicago's Englewood Station. My father awaited us, looking "like death warmed over", my mother was in tears and our future most uncertain.

2

Transition to American Education

On a cold winter morning in early 1937 an American cousin took me to Hyde Park High School and deposited me in the office of the Assistant Principal, Mr. Smalley, so I could register for the Spring semester. At this time, relatively few refugees had arrived at the school. On the basis of a number of examinations administered by the staff, I was given a substantial number of credits in French, German, Latin, History, and mathematics so that I could have graduated from high school at age 15 if it had not been for the fact that was I lacking credits in English, American History and civics. Clearly, German Gymnasium education had put me at least two or three years ahead of American students of the same age.

What I gained academically through my German education was offset, however, by a lack of social adjustment by American standards. My first year in an American high school brought difficulties, some of which were not funny at the time but with hindsight are humorous. After having taken all the exams, I was assigned to what in Chicago was referred to as a senior division room, more commonly referred to as a "homeroom". I sat in this room while an elderly teacher handed out slips of paper to various students and performed various record-keeping functions. I was still wondering what the meaning of "division" was in the context of a classroom. To me it simply meant an arithmetic operation. After about a half hour in homeroom, a bell rang and students "divided," i.e., ran in every direction. I just sat there not knowing what to do. Miss Johnson, the division room teacher, came up to me and said, "You had better hurry or you will be tardy." The word "tardy" was new to me and I had to consult my pocket dictionary, creating consternation in Miss Johnson's mind. She asked to see my program. To me a "program" was something one received at a theater performance. She pulled a slip of paper out of my hands and told me that in the next period (I thought a "period" was a type of punctuation) I was supposed to go to Room 242, which she explained to me was on the second floor of the west side of the building. I told her I could not know where the "west" side of the building was if I did not see the sun. At this point she must have thought I was completely crazy. I soon learned that only in America do people determine locations even inside buildings in terms of "north," "south," "east" and "west".

My German Gymnasium was for boys only, so adjusting to a coeducational setting at age 15 was difficult. American girls at age 17 are quite precocious by world standards. When I was the only one to arrive in homeroom wearing short pants, I stood out and was soon adopted as sort of a mascot. I had a lot of blond curls at the time and when the girls stroked my hair, I would turn red as a beet. It became a new sport for them to watch me blush.

Fortunately, some of our American relatives recognized these difficulties. I became equipped with long pants and was given dancing lessons which eased the necessary social adjustment.

It quickly became obvious that one of the greatest advantages of the American educational system over the German one was the type of personal relationships which existed between teachers and students. The American teacher is not only concerned with conveying knowledge, but watches the health and social adjustment of young people. Democratic participation by students through all sorts of clubs, student activities, student government and honor societies bring students and teachers together outside the classroom. This strengthen's the democratic attitudes which must be learned early in one's life.

However, I am convinced that there needs to be a compromise between the more rigorous academic emphasis so typical of European education and the possibly excessive American emphasis, especially in the lower grades, on play and social adjustment activities. I think that American children are "behind" academically up to the eighth grade. They begin to catch up in high school and unfortunately, after their first two years of college, are at least equal to the German high school graduate after 13 years of public school education.

One favorite example of teacher involvement regards my Hyde Park teacher, Walter Hipple. Although I had set a University of Chicago education as a personal objective, my parents could not begin to finance such an education even though we lived within walking distance and I would not need campus housing. Therefore, in 1938, I prepared intensely for the scholarship examination, which was given once a year and could be taken in three subject matter areas typically taught in high school. I chose history, French and German. Imagine my great disappointment when shortly before the scheduled exam date the University shifted from the three subject area examinations to a general achievement test covering the whole range of knowledge. I knew that my preparation in science was clearly inadequate. I was quite distraught. Fortunately, through Mr. Hipple's efforts, I was invited to visit the Director of Admissions and was given some scholarship assistance to begin my University studies. Through scholarships and assistantships, plus every conceivable type of part-time work from shining shoes, working in a warehouse, selling Fuller brushes from house to house, tutoring and selling in a retail store, I was able to complete both my undergraduate and graduate education without financial support from my parents, who steadfastly offered moral support along with room and board. Working one's way through college is uniquely American, an opportunity which contributes greatly to self-confidence and provides a "leg up" experience for the "real" world of work.

In recent years there has been much discussion in the United States about bilingual education. Advocates of what I see as excessive bilingual education feel that parents want to keep their children under their control by not permitting them to assimilate too quickly. This strikes me as a selfish attitude that in no way contributes to the child's success in a new environment. Other defendants are those rewarded by providing bilingual education, a particularly serious problem in American metropolitan areas that constitutes, in my judgment, a misallocation of resources for questionable objectives. Based on my own experience, I believe that much of this effort is misguided and damages immigrant children. Of course it is difficult for a child to transfer from one language to another and to adjust to a different cultural environment. Nevertheless, the younger the child the quicker the adjustment. In the long run the child will benefit from the absence of excessive coddling. Indeed, at most, bilingualism should occur for approximately six months after a child arrives in the American environment.

Lest my attitude on this subject be misunderstood, I must point out that I believe strongly in cultural pluralism and advocate the teaching of foreign languages and cultures. Children from Asian, European, or Latin American backgrounds have a potentially great advantage in preserving their own cultural heritage. But this should not be at the expense of becoming proficient in English or familiar with all aspects of American culture.

America has benefited tremendously from its "melting pot" society. It is increasingly an example of international and intercultural harmony. While it has a long way to go toward its tolerance of minority groups, this has in my opinion improved since World War II and is undoubtedly greater than in most other parts of the world.

Although I have had certain genetic and environmental advantages, I believe that my ability to acculturate rapidly is not unusual for a teenager. The American environment is receptive and the obstacles involved in the adjustment which an immigrant must overcome can also be of great benefit. There is little doubt in my mind that physical as well as cultural handicaps can be compensated for by motivation. To create such motivation, of course, requires an adequate support system. A strong family structure is an essential prerequisite to attain this objective. For example, I firmly believe that it is the high value placed on family support that explains the great success of Asian immigrants in recent years.

3

Higher Education—
The American Way

Robert Maynard Hutchins will undoubtedly be recognized in the history of American higher education as one its most seminal thinkers and most controversial administrators. To have been a student in the College of the University of Chicago in 1939 meant being caught up in the ferment of educational innovation largely initiated by Hutchins. Moreover, it was during this period that the great ideological conflicts of Europe were being fought out on American soil.

Whereas European higher education before World War II was almost exclusively specialized and professional, American higher education at the undergraduate level followed the English tradition of providing approximately two years of basic liberal arts education. What made the University of Chicago different from most other institutions during the Hutchins era was the fact that the curriculum in the College had very few options and all students were exposed to the major fields of knowledge, i.e., the humanities, the social sciences, the biological sciences and the physical sciences. All the students in the College had, in fact, done some of the same reading, observed the same scientific demonstrations and participated in discussions of the same topics with outstanding discussion leaders. Moreover, Hutchins insisted on having some of the University's greatest scholars give lectures to freshmen and sophomores. Exposure to these world-renowned individuals at age 17 or 18 was an experience that was bound to create high morale among students and resulted in lifelong nostalgia among University of Chicago alumni.

Much of the faculty was opposed to Hutchin's occasionally high-handed and autocratic approach to administration. Not all scholars wanted to "waste their time" lecturing to freshmen. After the 1960s it would become unthinkable for a university president to impose faculty members, no matter how talented, on a division or department without its concurrence. Hutchins made many controversial appointments of this nature, including that of Mortimer Adler to a professorship in the Law School. Adler and Hutchins were close ideologically and jointly presided over a quite popular seminar with a Thomist bent.

One of the appointments made during this period which greatly distressed a number of faculty members, particularly those of Jewish background, was that of Professor Arnold Bergstrasser to the Department of German. Opposition was led by a few senior members of the faculty, including Professor Louis Wirth, the world-renowned sociologist. The Bergstrasser appointment raises the interesting question of how far academic freedom extends. Does it go beyond the generally accepted concept of freedom of expression for those who are members of an academic community, or does it extend to the right of appointment of an individual whose past behavior or moral values can be questioned? As I recall the Bergstrasser case, no one questioned his competence or scholarship as a "Germanist". However, in the early '30s, Bergstrasser spoke in London at an international conference of philologists and had very kind words to say, according to the documents circulated at the University of Chicago, about Goebbels and the new German religion espoused by the Nazi ideologue Alfred Rosenberg. Nevertheless, in spite of the faculty opposition, Bergstrasser was appointed to the German Department. He apparently had had a "falling out" with the German regime in the later '30s. While he went to great lengths after arriving on the campus to befriend some Jewish students, there always remained a question about his sympathies.

In my own mind, and I never knew Bergstrasser personally, the appointment was further clouded by the fact that the chairperson of the Department of German at the time was a woman named Professor Gamer. I remember visiting her office in 1939 or 1940 because I was trying to obtain credits for my background in German. I was terribly shocked and dismayed that she had a photograph of Hitler prominently displayed in her office. I heard from others that she supposedly justified this display as "culturally appropriate" because Hitler was the head of state at the time. This explanation was unacceptable to me both rationally and emotionally.

One of Hutchins's wonderful innovations was the fact that all courses in the College culminated in a comprehensive examination. Students could take as many of these examinations as they wished. Moreover, because the tuition at the time was fixed at $100 per quarter or $300 per academic year, it was possible for a student to accelerate graduation from the two-year College via independent study. A number of students, including myself, took advantage of this opportunity to cut tuition expense—no doubt the reason the system was later changed.

In the late '30s the United States was just emerging from serious depression. Franklin Roosevelt's deficit financing at a time of large unemployment and the stimulus that came from the defense buildup contributed to the recovery. Nevertheless, jobs were still difficult to get and it was not always easy for a student to find part-time employment in order to finance an education. My parents, eager for me to succeed, sacrificed by providing room and board and other necessities, but it was incumbent on me to provide funds for tuition, books and incidentals. Fortunately for an immigrant, the American system favored the concept of "working your way through school." Although this was often difficult, there is enormous merit in having one foot in the academic community and the other in the real world. Being able to earn a living even under adverse circumstances contributes greatly to one's self-image and self-confidence. Work for even the most uneducated people who are engaged in unskilled labor has a democratizing effect which can be beneficial if good fortune enables one later in life to attain a managerial position.

As mentioned in the previous chapter, I began my education at the University of Chicago in February of 1939 with scholarship aid. Between 1939 and 1942, the year in which I received my bachelor's degree, I had to forego participation in extracurricular activities so popular with American students. During the academic year, I worked at part-time jobs, including a stint in a haberdashery store and a job teaching immigrants English, a language I myself had just mastered, and preparing them for the mandated citizenship examination. I had as many as fifteen students a week and was paid the "magnificent" sum of fifty cents per lesson. Among my students was the Nobel Laureate, Professor James Franck, who formerly had taught at the University of Göttingen and who was significantly involved in the research that developed nuclear fission at the University of Chicago.

During the summer of my undergraduate years, I worked full-time to finance my tuition for the following academic year. In 1939 I was a locker room attendant at the Idlewild Country Club in Flossmoor, Illinois. This involved scraping muddy golf shoes and shining elegant street footwear as well as mopping the floors and serving drinks. Working at the Club was quite a learning experience. I had never realized, given my sheltered upbringing, how much alcohol people consumed, nor was I fully aware of the consequences. My rather religious grandmother had always told me as a child that "Jews don't get drunk." I soon was disabused of this belief. My pay of $30 a month plus room and board would have been insufficient; however, my weekend tips for carrying golf bags to people's cars late at night enabled me to double my monthly income.

On various occasions my University of Chicago classmates were among the guests at the Club. Given my persistent German pride, I was somewhat embarrassed about my menial tasks. Only later did I realize that my lifestyle was in the finest American tradition and not something about which I should feel ashamed. Working at the club was my first opportunity to become familiar with the "culture" of upper income Americans. Learning something of the language of the golf course was most helpful several years later when I became President of Roosevelt University.

In my sophomore summer I worked in the warehouse of a large Chicago department store chain—Goldblatt Brothers. Because finding a summer job was often difficult, I learned early in my career the importance of what we now call "networking". My warehouse assignment was to fill the orders for approximately ten different stores in the Goldblatt chain. I worked in the tobacco and novelties department but fortunately never succumbed to the smoking temptation. Every Monday I lived with the fear of losing my job, because this was a period of retrenchment. At the beginning of each week some people who reported to work did not find their "time card" in the rack. I was fortunate to lose only a few days of work during that summer because we went out on a "sympathy strike" for the benefit of a handful of electricians who were making much more money than the order fillers. The electricians received a hefty raise a few days later and most of us got "docked" for the period we were out on strike. Clearly, we had made a sacrifice for the aristocracy of labor.

This was the only time in my life that I worked with a union card. In order to keep my Goldblatt's job, I had to join the upholsterers' union even though tobacco was certainly unrelated to sofas or easy chairs. My summer experience in the warehouse also led to a part-time selling job at Christmastime in Goldblatt's flagship department store.

In my junior year, I moved up in the world, managing to get a white collar job as a house-to-house salesman for the Fuller Brush Company. I was a member of a team of University of Chicago students that was moved into various Chicago neighborhoods where sales were lagging. No sociology course could have taught me more about Chicago's various neighborhoods. I worked in the rooming house neighborhoods with three or four names listed on every door bell, and in nice octagonal-front bungalow communities of Bohemian ethnicity. I learned to fear barking dogs and the problems of nondeliverable inventory and nonpayment for merchandise. I learned about marketing and the importance of a positive attitude. Setting goals and accomplishing them became a realistic necessity. No matter how difficult selling was on certain days, I never stopped making calls until I had reached my day's sales goal. It has been clear to me ever since that one can succeed only by being optimistic and upbeat. People do not buy out of sympathy. This lesson was carried over into my fundraising activity at Roosevelt: if the cause is good, convince people that they are faced with a great opportunity rather than plead out of pity.

When I reached my senior year, it was time to consider seriously my ultimate career objectives. Although history has always been among my major interests, I was well advised to major in economics because the career opportunities would be greater with an economics degree rather than one in social sciences or humanities. In the late '30s and '40s, a work-study program was established as part of the New Deal. Under the auspices of the National Youth Administration (NYA), funds were allocated to colleges and universities for the part-time employment of needy students. I was fortunate to secure an NYA assignment at the Cowles Commission for Research in Economics, then affiliated with the University of Chicago. At the time of my appointment, the Cowles Commission was being directed by Professor Theodore Yntema, who later became a vice president for finance at the Ford Motor Company. My menial activity consisted primarily of using an old-fashioned Monroe Calculator in connection with time series studies of stock market performances. (Many of these laborious calculations could now be done by computer in a matter of minutes.)

My interesting academic contacts in the Economics Department and at the Cowles Commission made me want very much to go on to graduate school, although for financial reasons I could not see how to accomplish this objective. I began a job search and, based on my interest in taxation, I had reached the second interview stage in the tax department of Sears Roebuck and Company, at the time unquestionably the largest merchandising operation in the world. Returning to the University Social Science Building after the interview, I was stopped in the hall by one of the Economics professors, who wanted to know what it would take to keep me at the University to do graduate work. Needless to say, my tongue was hanging out for any opportunity to stay in school. I was immensely pleased when I was told that the Cowles Commission had received a major grant to study the impact of price control and rationing on the American economy. I was offered a research assistantship involving approximately 30 hours per week. This arrangement enabled me to take graduate courses and included a tuition voucher to finance my education. I was overjoyed. At this time, the Cowles Commission received new leadership: Professor Jacob J. Marschak became the director of the Commission and George Katona, a Hungarian refugee, was put in charge of the price control project on which I worked from 1942 to 1944 while completing my course work for my doctorate in economics.

When the United States entered World War II in December 1941, I was highly eager to do my part in the war effort. The defeat of Hitler was an issue of world significance as well as a very personal concern. Twice I was classified 1A. Despite my efforts to convince the ophthalmologists that I could perform important work for the military, I was continually rejected for my poor eyesight. Although this rejection provided me with an educational opportunity many of my peers lacked, I considered it a great personal blow to my ego. Moreover, I had to overcome the ridiculous classification as an enemy alien. Not until 1944 could I obtain the much coveted U.S. citizenship.

The price control study, the wider contact with faculty members at the University of Chicago, my developing professional contacts and participation in Cowles Commission seminars enabled me to mature as a scholar and strengthened my resolve to enter the teaching profession. During this period I made an interesting contact at a party at George Kantona's home. Among the guests was Leo Szilard, who later became a famous nuclear scientist and who, together with Einstein, was instrumental in convincing Franklin Roosevelt to give the highest priority to atomic research. As Szilard and I talked, I asked him about his work at the University. He told me of his interest in metallurgy, but was unreceptive to my further inquiries about metallurgy not being a recognized University discipline. I arrived at the erroneous conclusion that he was an arrogant windbag, only to discover later that I had made an embarrassing inquiry about this great man's super-secret activity.

In 1944 I saw a communication in the Cowles Commission office indicating that the price control project was not going to be funded again. No one had told me about this officially, but my concern led me to look for a professional position that would coincide with my interests and that would enable me to remain in Chicago to complete my doctoral work. Based on my interest in public finance and my fairly close involvement with Professor Simeon Leland, who was the Economics Department chair and professor of public finance, I decided to apply for a position in the property tax division of the Illinois Department of Revenue. This division, prior to a reorganization, had been known as the Illinois Tax Commission, where Leland had been an influential commissioner. Some of the best economists in Chicago had been or were presently involved with the theoretical work in the field of tax assessments and valuations being conducted by this agency. I was thrilled when they offered me a research analyst position and happily gave fair notice to my employers at the Cowles Commission. A few days later I was dismayed and disillusioned to learn that my supervisor at the University had called the Department of Revenue and told them that I was "indispensable." He asked them to delay my appointment by several months, to which they agreed. I was obviously "over a barrel." I complained bitterly to Dr. Marschak about what I considered unethical conduct only to be told that "one does not get very far in the United States by practicing Kantian ethics." That statement from a German scholar was indeed hard to take.

By the time of my departure from my Alma Mater, I had completed all the course work for the doctorate and during the period of my employment with the Illinois Department of Revenue, I had taken the three written preliminary examinations for the doctorate. I passed them all at the required level and was awarded my master's degree from the University of Chicago in 1945. The commencement enabled me to combine two events at one time. On March 23, 1945, I not only received my master's degree, but more importantly celebrated my engagement to Leni

Metzger, whom I married that November.

While I was working at the Illinois Department of Revenue, I began my teaching career. The University of Chicago Economics Department recommended that I teach part-time at Indiana University in East Chicago, Indiana. I taught economics there for approximately three years beginning in 1945. Also, one of my colleagues at the Department of Revenue was teaching part-time at the Central YMCA College and occasionally I substituted for him in a statistics course. Having tutored as an undergraduate and having taught large classes at Indiana, I felt increasingly confident about becoming a successful college teacher. I was very eager to teach full time. But I also felt that I should spend a reasonable period of time at the Department of Revenue. So it was not until 1946 that I became connected with the fledgling Roosevelt College and embarked on my long career at this institution.

The most fascinating aspect of my work at the Department of Revenue was my involvement in the implementation of property tax reform legislation commonly referred to in Illinois as the Butler Laws. These laws provided for intercounty property tax equalization through the use of assessment to sales ratio methodology. I was in charge of the statistical work connected with this reform. Not only did this research enable me to develop considerable expertise in tax administration, but it also taught me some important political lessons and helped me to overcome a degree of idealistic naivete.

Based on elaborate and sophisticated calculations, we arrived at "multipliers," which were to equalize the level of assessments for Illinois' 102 counties. Clearly, the multiplier had much to do with the distribution of tax burdens and was, therefore, a politicaly "hot potato." I soon found that statistically accurate calculations would be corrected by politically appointed policy makers and I remember distinctly asking the director of revenue why my numbers had been changed after I had checked and rechecked them for accuracy. The "enlightening" response from the director confirmed my fear of political intrusion. He stated simply that statistical calculations, which could not be completely accurate, had to be modified by the "mature judgment" of a top policy-making official responsible to the governor. It became very evident that in the inflationary period of the '40s, the director of revenue was determined to keep the multipliers affection local property assessments in check, thereby increasing the relative burden of state assessed railroad property and simultaneously keeping down the taxing power of thousands of school districts which were facing rapid enrollment increases.

Although I thoroughly enjoyed working with my colleagues, who were among the country's top property tax experts, I realized that working for politicians "at the top" was not for me. However, the experience of visiting counties and talking with the local power structure was extremely valuable training in the essence of democracy: the art of surviving in the world of conflicting interests by resolving problems through discussion and negotiation.

My determination to leave the civil service and to enter full-time teaching was further stimulated by an event during the 1946 spring campaign. I was solicited for a financial contribution for the governor's war chest. I had been warned about this and had looked up the pertinent provision in the Illinois statutes which clearly indicated that the solicitation of civil service employees constituted a felony. When a department attorney came to see me for my contribution, I pointed this out to him. He promptly proceed to give me a lecture on how my job could simply be abolished and why somebody who had never rung a doorbell should make political contributions to preserve the system which provided me with a "secure" appointment. I did not make a contribution and there were no further repercussions, but I decided it would be wise to search for a teaching job.

I had registered with the University of Chicago Placement Office and received all notifications of vacancies available in my field from around the country. It was distressing to learn that in the immediate postwar period, discrimination in appointments at the college level was rampant. There was nothing subtle about this. Vacancy announcements frequently indicated a preference for a person of a Christian religion and often made clear that a person of a college's denominational affiliation would receive preferential treatment. It was evident that as a Jew I would have great difficulty getting equal consideration at many institutions of higher learning, an extremely disillusioning situation in light of my adolescent years in Nazi Germany.

The prevalence of discrimination in the United States as late as the '40s became more evident on my honeymoon trip to the Smoky Mountains in November 1945. During a stopover in Knoxville, Tennessee, I saw park benches and washrooms designated "Whites Only." It was difficult to comprehend that such discrimination could exist in a democratic society. If there was discrimination against Jews, how much greater was it bound to be against blacks? Indeed, during the 1980s I often felt that the United States may be unduly self-righteous in its justified criticism of South Africa.

My experiences in Germany and the more subtle prejudices that existed in the United States made me eager to develop a connection with a new college which was about to be founded in Chicago. In early 1945, on a train trip from East Chicago to Hyde Park, I had conversed with two faculty colleagues, Otto Wirth, a Germanist, and Lionel Ruby, a philosopher, about the revolt at the Central YMCA College of Chicago, led by Edward J. Sparling. He was going to split from the old institution to establish a college based on equal educational opportunity regardless of race or creed. Otto Wirth said he had already signed a contract there and was going to join the new faculty. He spoke enthusiastically about the ideals of the institution and an innovative concept of culture studies he planned to introduce. I was intrigued and hoped at some future time I might join this faculty with its "utopian" mission.

Coincidentally, the opportunity to work at Roosevelt College came sooner than anticipated. In December of 1945 I decided to attend the annual meeting of the American Economic Association in Cleveland, Ohio. On the train trip back to Chicago, I was grading a set of economic examinations. A rather attractive, tall gentleman sat down next to me and struck up a conversation. I had seen him before at the Cowles Commission seminar and he re-introduced himself as Professor Walter Weisskopf, Chairman of the Economics Department at Roosevelt College. With the kind of self-deprecating honesty which I found later to be characteristic of Walter, he wondered whether he could have a copy of my exam. As he put it, "I am lazy about such things as preparing tests and maybe I can adapt yours to my needs." I was glad to give him a copy. We learned that we had much in common. He was originally from Vienna and also a refugee from the Nazis. He told me a good deal about the new college, about its democratic governance and about the number of refugee scholars that had found an intellectual home in the center of Chicago. He asked whether I would be willing to teach part-time at Roosevelt. I politely declined since I saw no reason for changing part-time positions. However, I made it clear that I would seriously consider a full-time opportunity. He said he would keep me in mind but that vacancies would depend on enrollments and that the institution was totally tuition dependent and operating on a shoestring.

Imagine my surprise, during the summer of 1946, to receive a call from Walter Weisskopf telling me that because of enroll-ment growth at Roosevelt an additional appointment in econom-ics was needed. Could I come in to see Wayne A.R. Leys, the Dean of Arts and Sciences, as well as the Academic Vice President of the College? Leys and I "hit it off" immediately. I was impressed by his intellectual capacity and the conduct of the interview. I was offered a three-year appointment as Assistant Professor of Eco-nomics at a salary of $3,000. This was an easy offer to accept for several reasons. I believed in the ideals of the institution and I very much liked the faculty members I had met, particularly Weisskopf and Wirth. Moreover, staying in Chicago was important to me. I could easily communicate with any doctoral committee at the University of Chicago while I completed my dissertation and, most importantly, I could remain close to my aging parents. I felt an obligation as an only son to remain near them and my wife shared by feelings. I signed a contract to start teaching at Roosevelt College in the fall of 1946, with the understanding that I could supplement by modest salary with overload teaching at Roosevelt College as well as continued part-time teaching at Indiana University. I was not quite 25 years old and I was full of ambition. Things had truly gone well. I was on my way towards the doctorate, I had a teaching position at a progressive institution in the city where I wanted to stay, and I had found a spouse who would continue to encourage me in my future endeavors.

Part II.

Portals to Opportunity

"Education makes a people easy to lead, but difficult to drive; easy to govern, but impossible to enslave."

Lord Henry Peter Brougham,
Scottish Statesman, 1778-1863

4

Roosevelt College—An American Experiment in Education

Political as well as educational revolutions have root causes. Those that have failed have done so because the timing was wrong, public support was inadequate or the underlying ideology did not find acceptance.

The history of the Central YMCA College of Chicago included both an aborted and a successful revolution. In the '30s the Central YMCA College faculty became restless. The College had had considerable success in performing a major function contemplated for it by the YMCA of Greater Chicago. The objective was to provide higher educational opportunities for working people in the city. The College was set up to provide day and evening classes and had always accepted full- and part-time students when colleges and universities were not receptive to the education of the part-time adult student. Moreover, during the depression of the '30s, the Central YMCA College was able to attract an unusually talented faculty at relatively low pay compared to the prevailing salary scales. The faculty had a heavy teaching load and performed an unusually large number of semi-clerical duties in addition to their teaching. Many of them were excellent scholars who, in addition to their heavy teaching loads, were able to publish in their chosen fields.

They were greatly distressed, however, by the perception that the YMCA had not raised endowment or other significant funds for the College, had diverted cash flow from the College to other possibly worthy endeavors and lacked an understanding of academic administration. An effort to break away from the YMCA was defeated and resulted in the dismissal of the leadership of the revolt. Emery Balduf, who had been dean of the College, and Millard Everett, his deputy, lost their positions. (They would become members of the new Roosevelt College faculty and administration.) Although the faculty of the Central YMCA College may have had many "bread and butter" grievances and limited administrative autonomy, it became clear that the power structure of the YMCA could only stem the revolt by surrendering to the dissident faculty. Depressed economic conditions and the absence of a new educational philosophy or ideology can be considered as reasons for this failure.

Although the YMCA forces that defeated the resolution were still in control at the end of World War II, two factors contributed to the amazing success of the faculty revolt in 1945. The first was the presence of Edward J. Sparling as president of the College. The second was a change in the American value system, not yet clearly understood by large segments of American society and brought about by World War II. America's large citizen army and the victorious fight against dictatorship and discrimination in Europe had laid the groundwork for a fundamental shift toward broader and more meaningful democracy.

While it may have been the YMCA's objective to preserve the status quo with an emphasis on assisting Christian men and women in attaining an education in a "comfortable" environment, (although never publicly stated) it was the consensus of many of the faculty members that the YMCA wanted to guard against an "excessive" number of non-white or non-Christian students in its enrollment mix.

It was in this context that the YMCA Board requested Jim Sparling to provide demographic data for policy-making purposes. Sparling frequently stated his belief that the only purpose for this request was to consider some form of quota system. This was emphatically denied by members of the Board, including Stanley Harris, Sr., who until that date had been Sparling's close friend and mentor. The overwhelming majority of staff members, however, rallied to Sparling's side on this issue, which they saw as a test of their democratic ideology, although in many cases the motivation also included materialistic and programmatic considerations.

In addition to the dispute over potential racial discrimination, there were serious personality clashes related to President Sparling's strongly held views regarding other social and economic issues. His active support of trade unions, New Deal social policies and concepts of world government did not "sit well" with the power structure of the YMCA, which was essentially conservative. And although a large number of faculty members were in agreement with Sparling's ideological position, an even larger number objected to the lack of autonomy of the College and the interference with academic freedom.

If the YMCA had agreed, as had been repeatedly suggested, to separate the College from the total control by the YMCA of Greater Chicago, the College could have continued with its YMCA affiliation. This was, however, not to be. The courage and determination of Sparling to undertake the risky founding of a new institution resulted in his "resignation under protest" and a rallying of "liberal" forces in the community around the concept of an urban college devoted to equal educational opportunity regardless of race or creed.

Edward "Jim" Sparling was a charismatic leader, full of idealism and with a stubborn streak that enabled him to pursue his goals even against great odds. He was the right person at the right time.

It was the support of Marshall Field III, the publisher of the *Chicago Sun;* the Rosenwald Fund, under the chairmanship of Edwin R. Embree; the union movement and the small number of progressive individuals such as Leo Lerner, publisher of a chain of community newspapers; Percy Julian, a noted black scientist, Harland Allen, an investment counselor; Floyd J. Reeves, a professor of educational administration at the University of Chicago; and John McGrath, editor of the *Chicago Sun,* that made the establishment of the new College in April 1945 a reality. Edwin Embree became the first Board chairman and Allen, Lerner, Julian, McGrath, Reeves, and Sparling were the founding Board. Although the initial charter was issued in the name of Thomas Jefferson College, the death of Franklin Delano Roosevelt in April 1945 resulted in the adoption of his name.

Although with the passage of time Roosevelt has become quite a satisfactory name, it did not help the institution in its early years when the word Roosevelt brought out extremely hostile responses among the conservative establishment. Indeed, this hostility made it difficult for the founders of the College to raise funds from the corporate sector. Even though a painful estrangement occurred between Sparling and Stanley Harris, Sr., his former mentor, it is interesting to note that after I became President of Roosevelt University it was possible, with the assistance of our Board Chairman Lyle Spencer, to get a substantial gift from the Harris Bank. Stanley Harris, Jr., who had been taught how to swim as a child by Jim Sparling, told me in making a gift to Roosevelt in the late '60s that it was time to let bygones be bygones. Some years later his sister, Cynthia Harris, became a supporter of the University and a member of the President's Club, one of the University's giving groups.

Educational Democracy and Faculty Participation

The founders of Roosevelt College were determined to set up an administrative framework which would provide protection against Board interference in the formulation of academic policy and which would shift power distribution very substantially from the lay Board to the faculty. There would be faculty members on the Board of Trustees and votes of confirmation and votes of confidence on the deans and the president would be taken by secret ballot from a constituency consisting of part-time as well as full-time faculty and administration. It was the initial intention of the framers of the College bylaws and faculty constitution to have half the Board elected by the faculty. Fortunately, the faculty recognized that such a degree of faculty control over the Board might create serious fundraising limitations. As a result, the number of elected faculty members was limited to five, not more than two of whom could be members of the administration. Faculty representation therefore comprised twenty-five percent of the Board.

A comprehensive discussion of faculty trusteeship in higher

education, with special reference to Roosevelt, can be found in the work of Daniel H. Perlman.* Dr. Perlman concluded from his study of the 1945 events that, although Sparling favored the original proposal of ten elected faculty members on a Board of twenty members plus the college president, ex officio, he was satisfied with the compromise.

Moreover, it was clear that the objections raised by Floyd Reeves, a lay Board member and a recognized expert on educational administration, had some impact on both the president and the faculty. Although the Perlman study on balance supports the benefits derived from faculty participation on the Board, I think it would have been preferable for the faculty to recommend Board members to a Board nominating committee, which then could have selected faculty representatives from a faculty proposed slate. The concern of the faculty, as expressed in one of the early meetings, was related to administrative representation. This issue was resolved by limiting administrative representation to two members.

Three decades later there developed an unwillingness on the part of the faculty to elect any administrators to the Board. Because it is important for the president to have some administrators present at Board meetings as resource persons, this system resulted in the vice presidents for business and development, as well as the director of public relations, sitting in on Board meetings without a vote. This, of course, made for even greater "in house" representation at Board meetings. Since faculty and administrative staff have an excellent attendance record, they constituted a greater percentage of those present at meetings than was contemplated. Although public Board members respect faculty, the nature of the group dynamic is changed considerably with a questionable impact on Board behavior.

In spite of the great fervor and esprit de corps of the first two

---

*Daniel H. Perlman: "Faculty Trusteeship in Higher Education—A Study of the Governance of Roosevelt University," U.S. Department of Health, Education, and Welfare; Office of Education; Bureau of Research.

years of Roosevelt College, the unified sense of purpose could not be expected to last and major controversies began to arise very early. Democracy is a concept that is viewed very differently by political theorists and by faculty. What is meant by democratic governance of an educational institution varies. At one extreme, an institution can have faculty "legislation" on all college issues with equal votes for all. At the other extreme, faculty participation can be limited to consultation on issues with faculty decision-making essentially confined to issues of tenure and promotion. (A further option is for a college to have a system of "representative" governance, a compromise between no participation and full voting rights for all.)

Roosevelt College started out with a faculty that was an all-inclusive voting body, meaning full-time administrators and all full-time and part-time faculty could vote. Because part-time faculty did not typically depend on their meager Roosevelt College salary for their livelihood, they were present at faculty meetings only when pressed to do so by department chairs or others who were vitally interested in an issue. They were frequently used to "pack" the house. Administrators as well as teaching faculty debated the need for change in 1947-48. The first debate dealt with the elimination of votes for part-time faculty, which was the least controversial issue. The hotly debated issue was the shift to a "representative" form of faculty governance, with representation of departments dependent on size and calculated by a rarely understood formula developed by the Mathematics Department. Even more bitter was the debate over administrative representation. The founding administrators believed that there should be "unity"—that not unlike the statement of Louis XIV that "l'etat c'est moi," they felt that "the faculty: it is us." They were sincere but unrealistic in their expectations. As a result the revised constitution designated by position the administrators who would become *ex officio* members of the newly established senate. Nondesignated administrators were to elect a representative to the senate.

One of the unavoidable tragedies related to democratic

governance is the inordinate amount of time that is diverted from substantive discussion of academic issues to politics centering on procedural matters. The new constitution of the faculty was debated publicly and in caucus settings for many months and diverted energies from what with hindsight were undoubtedly more urgent concerns.

The most bitter controversy in those early days of constitutional debate on governance related to the question of whether majority rule or preferential voting should be used. Faculty members viewed themselves as James Madisons, or other heroes depending on their own political ideology. No matter how learned a faculty member was, he or she may be susceptible to a fundamental confusion, if not an intentional misunderstanding, about the difference between a democratic state (requiring extreme safeguards for civil liberties) and the nonprofit institution which, although not a business in the usual sense, must be able to make decisions promptly without excessive and emasculating compromises.

Almost all of the administrators were "majority vote" advocates. On the faculty side this view was vigorously presented by the more conservative element in the faculty and by an outstanding neo-Kantian, Professor Siegfried Marck, who had been an *ordinarius* professor at the University of Breslau before fleeing from the Nazis in the thirties. Marck made the potent argument against proportional representation, i.e., that it leads to excessive factionalism, can be used to pervert majority positions, and enables extreme influences to gain a foothold. Obviously, he was much influenced by his political experiences during the ill-fated Weimar Republic. Those who advocated the preferential system of voting included many idealistic young faculty members, myself included. We were greatly influenced by the prevalent civil liberties arguments. With hindsight and much administrative experience I am convinced that this argument was greatly flawed and I attribute my position at the time to my immaturity. Nevertheless, the preferential ballot won out and the College (later the University) has had to live with the consequences of this

1948 decision. It has resulted from time to time in blocks concentrating their votes while the politically uninitiated dispersed their votes. As a result militant groups were able to gain control of committees at times of agitation. Furthermore, this voting system was never fully understood by a majority of faculty and vote counting has typically been handled by mathematicians and political scientists.

Academic Freedom and the Cold War

At the same time that the new constitution was debated, American politics of the late '40s and early '50s were preoccupying the faculty and administration. The circumstances surrounding the founding of the College created major public relations problems. The nondiscrimination policy, the pro-union posture, and the FDR name all combined to create the unwarranted perception of an anti-business attitude on the part of the young institution. Moreover, being for civil rights, establishing a labor education division, and getting important, even if less than adequate, support from a "liberal" heavily Jewish constituency all contributed to the myth of Roosevelt College being a "little red schoolhouse", i.e., a place that welcomed and harbored Communists.

Actually, the faculty of Roosevelt College was essentially "middle of the road" politically. The Board, administration and faculty were overwhelmingly progressive regarding issues of racial and religious discrimination and the majority were supportive of President Roosevelt's "New Deal" policies. On economic issues and in social relationships the faculty continued to reflect its YMCA origins. It was particularly distressing to the founding faculty that the school had the undeserved reputation of being "pink."

Therefore, in the late '40s, a split developed in the faculty between those who belonged to a "conservative" caucus and those who joined the so-called "liberal" caucus. Starting in 1947 the "conservatives," to protect the reputation of the new institution, wanted to purge it of people that might be regarded as "fellow travelers." As a new faculty member, I was greatly distressed by what I considered a "witch hunt" in the making. Self-appointed experts, including former Trotskyites who claimed special expertise, issued lists of faculty and clerical staff members who ought to be "eliminated" from the employment roster or who at least required close watching. Our "experts" on the anti-communist left were such driven individuals that they allied themselves with a handful of arch-conservatives to attain their objectives. I suspect, however, that only two clerical employees lost their jobs as a result of all this.

But the tenor of the time created much more serious threats to academic freedom nationally with local repercussions. Walter McCarran and Joseph McCarthy began to exert influence in the Congress and started anti-communist investigations, which in the Illinois legislature were imitated by Senator Broyles. Because a substantial number of people, among them University of Chicago and Roosevelt College students, went to Springfield early in 1949 to demonstrate against the Broyles bills which sought to outlaw communism in Illinois, the two schools were singled out by the Illinois Seditious Activities Investigating Commission for special consideration. President Hutchins of the University of Chicago and President Sparling of Roosevelt College testified effectively before the Commission and the matter died. The Broyles bills were never brought to the floor for a vote.

Votes of Confirmation and Confidence

A discussion of Roosevelt College as an experiment in American higher education is not complete without a brief historical outline of votes of confirmation and confidence on deans as well as on the president. Votes of confirmation of new appointments had to take place by the end of the first year of an administrator's tenure and votes of confidence were taken every three years on the president and on the deans. This concept, which had been written into the faculty constitution, was supported broadly by the founding faculty and administration because of their utopian impulses and their idealism. As often expressed by Jim Sparling, they believed they were the "Roosevelt family." That the success of the new institution was the common interest and objective of all segments of the institution tended to blind the writers of the constitution to the reality of inherent conflicts of interest that develop between faculty, staff and top administration and to the fact that rapid growth of an institution soon eliminates the "family" feeling. In later years Sparling admitted that the institutionalization of these votes was a mistake he regretted.

Votes of confirmation lasted into the 1950s, when the faculty was easily convinced that they had to be eliminated. Whereas promotions to deanships from within the College provided no serious obstacles, outsiders were reluctant to relocate if they were to be subjected to a vote after one year, not to mention the triennial vote of confidence.

Votes of confidence became a much more serious issue. It can be argued that a regular vote of confidence by secret ballot provides a guaranteed system of evaluation of the president and the deans and provides guidance to the Board regarding the president and to the president with regard to his academic administrators. Although the votes were advisory, they were announced at faculty and board meetings and published in the minutes and in the student newspaper. Faculty members felt that this was an important empowerment—a feeling I strongly shared in my teaching days.

It is not surprising, however, that after seven years of administrative experience as a dean and twenty-three years as President I changed my mind. To understand fully the psychological impact of the votes, I must describe the process: the dean or the president had to request the vote every third year. The appropriate executive committee would appoint three faculty members to conduct the vote. A black box would be set up in the president's office for votes of confidence on deans and in the Dean of Faculties' office for presidential votes. Voting took place during a one- to two-week period.

Unfortunately, this system often led to highly politicized unhealthy campaigns. A small number of faculty members enjoyed reminding deans in joking or threatening ways that they would have a chance to vote on them. Although, with only two exceptions in forty years, votes resulted in over fifty percent affirmation, the atmosphere literally incapacitated some deans, preventing them from functioning administratively for almost six months prior to a vote. Even though many deans said they could not be intimidated, some hesitated to make tough decisions at crucial times. I found it unreasonable to expect most administrators to feel at ease in such an atmosphere. A personal experience illustrates my point. My appointment to the presidency took place in October and therefore I requested my vote in October of the appropriate years. One of my faculty antagonists made an issue of this timetable, arguing in the faculty senate for spring votes because fall votes did not allow the faculty time to "organize." The senate accepted his argument.

Although I very much agreed with Sparling's conclusion that the negatives of votes of confidence outweighed the advantages, I did not wish to create debilitating internal friction during my term of office any more than he had during his presidency. Depending on one's point of view, this may be considered cowardice or prudence. A major stumbling block was the requirement of a two-thirds vote of the senate or a majority vote in an all-faculty referendum to amend the faculty constitution. To complicate the issue further, the bylaws did not give the Board the power to change the faculty constitution.

In 1964 a consulting report by the firm of Cresap, McCormick and Paget recommended abolishing votes of confidence along with other innovations of democratic governance. A later chapter will explain how the tenor of this report was unfortunate and the timing inappropriate. Public Board members frequently discussed this issue but neither the president nor the Board wished to tackle a matter which would be divisive and possibly destructive of morale. The opportunity for abolishing the vote finally arose during my last year in office. The presidential search committee was advised by the search consultant that the vote of confidence provision would conceivably eliminate good candidates for the position. As a result the Board changed the bylaws so as to make votes of confidence inconsistent with the bylaws. The timing was right and the action, which I had considered appropriate for many years, was finally feasible.

Should there ever be votes of confidence? In an extreme crisis a president or a dean might ask for such a vote. Or the faculty might demand the same under unusual circumstances. Such votes, however, should never be institutionalized. While it is true that after a strong and positive vote of confidence, a president or dean feels greatly strengthened in executing a mandate, on a regular basis these votes can become detrimental popularity contests. This participatory governance experiment at Roosevelt failed. It demonstrates all too clearly the danger of carrying too far the analogy between a university and the state.

5

Postwar Boom – Growth and Opportunity

A College Becomes A University 1945-1960

The founding of Roosevelt College in 1945 was based on both a moral imperative and fortuitous circumstances. As the war wound down, policymakers became concerned about the economic impact of the huge manpower pool that would be released from the military and the defense establishment.

The desire to provide equity and justice for those who had sacrificed several years of their lives for their country led to the enactment of the GI Bill of Rights. Never before and never since has the United States undertaken a broader or more generous act for educational entitlement. The Bill provided for tuition payments as well as subsistence allowances. For the first time in American history, educational opportunity became a meaningful option for a broad cross-section of Americans regardless of race, religion or economic class. The two difficulties created by this massive expansion were a lack of adequate educational facilities, particularly in urban areas, and a still prevalent prejudice against minority groups and part-time students.

Chicago was typical of the demand pressures created by the college population explosion. During the first few years of Roosevelt's existence, Chicago's educational needs were met by the University of Chicago, Northwestern, Loyola and DePaul universities, two Chicago teachers colleges and Roosevelt. The first two of these universities, recognized as national research institutions, were only a minor factor in meeting the city's educational needs. Undergraduate education for the broad spectrum of Chicagoans, including the large number of GIs, became the obligation of DePaul, Loyola and Roosevelt. Because DePaul and Loyola were strictly Catholic universities, Roosevelt became the only nonsectarian institution serving the needs of higher education for a heterogeneous student body.

It is not surprising, therefore, that when Roosevelt College, as a successor to the YMCA College, opened its doors in a hastily acquired old office building at 231 South Wells Street, it faced fantastic growth. Enrollment exploded from under 1,300 students to over 5,000 between 1945 and 1948, with approximately half studying under the GI Bill. Nor is it surprising that Roosevelt attracted a significant number of black and Jewish students, a large proportion of whom were the first members of their families to have the opportunity to go to college. They were a highly motivated group, eager to succeed and in a hurry to make up for lost time.

Referring to the objectives and underlying philosophy of Roosevelt, President Sparling said in his 1947-48 President's Report, "We do not mean to imply that equality of opportunity is the same thing as education for everybody but we have success-fully affirmed in practice the theory that all students who can profit by a college education should have the equal privilege of obtaining a college education."

It is difficult to do justice to the milieu that existed in Roosevelt's early days. The students came to an old, poorly furnished office building and waited patiently in long lines to register. Morale on the part of both students and faculty was high in spite of low salaries, crowded classrooms and scheduling problems. I doubt if any group of college administrators has ever performed more heroically under adverse circumstances than the Roosevelt College leadership: primarily Jim Sparling; Wayne A. R. Leys, the academic vice president; and Lowell Huelster, the vice president for business and finance. The institution started on a shoestring and literally operated from "hand-to-mouth." In order to meet the onslaught of students, faculty had to be hired before the income to pay their salaries was assured. Borrowing in anticipation of tuition receipts became a juggling act made more difficult by the prejudice against the new institution on the part of the banking community.

One innovative procedure developed to expedite registration was euphemistically referred to as "blue plate specials." Each of these "packages" was composed of a combination of five courses designed to meet the special needs of arts and sciences students, business students, exclusively day students, exclusively evening students, etc. Most of the students, particularly the GIs, were full-time, many eager to carry heavy overloads. Because not enough daytime classrooms were available many full-time students were forced to take evening classes. The enrollment increases that occurred in the early years enabled Roosevelt to become firmly established and fully accredited. According to U.S. Office of Education estimates, college enrollments increased nationally by 113 percent between the fall of 1945 and spring of 1947. For Roosevelt the increase was 221 percent.

The phenomenal enrollment increase was matched by budget and faculty growth between 1945 and 1949. For example, annual expenditures grew from an unbelievably small amount of $400,000 in fiscal year 1945-46, to about $2 million in 1948-49 when faculty and staff reached a total of 325.

The quality of the student body was above average, based on freshman scores on the then commonly used American Council on Education Tests. Furthermore, the ideology of the institution was to be truly "color blind" and judge people on merit only. While no exact data are available on the college's racial and ethnic composition because students were never asked to indicate race, religion or ethnicity on any records, the student body included a large Jewish component and Roosevelt became a prestige institution for black students. Indeed, it was quite difficult for me to adjust to the 1960s mentality resulting from the government's edict requiring us to keep records on race. In fact, we asked students to classify themselves anonymously by race at the time of registration.

Nondiscrimination was a tremendous asset for Roosevelt in

its early days because the institution was able to recruit a superb faculty in which minorities were heavily represented. Among the full-time faculty in 1946 were a substantial number of refugees from the Nazis, outstanding Afro-American scholars who could not find employment in traditional institutions and several Asians. The college was truly culturally pluralistic, politically and intellectually diverse, and could boast of a stimulating atmosphere that contrasted sharply with the predominant youth culture on small-town American campuses. While Roosevelt's curriculum was rather standard for the time, the college was a pioneer in the concept of the study of others as an alternative or supplement to language instruction. The importance of teaching about other cultures has not diminished over the years but unfortunately interest in such courses declined and as a result offerings were reduced after the 1950s. Ironically, Roosevelt could offer more and better courses dealing with Africa in 1950 than in 1980.

In spite of lean budgets, much institutional research was conducted at Roosevelt, using manual data collection now considered unthinkable in the computer age. One illustration suffices. Based on the overall quality of the students, the administration and faculty decided that approximately ten percent of all grades given should be As, twenty-five percent Bs, forty percent Cs, twenty percent Ds, and five percent Fs. We wanted neither grade inflation nor excessive severity. How was a professor to know whether he had an above or below average class? The registrar undertook an imaginative and useful regular study to provide guidelines for the faculty: Based on an averaging of aptitude scores, high school standing and previous grades at Roosevelt, students were statistically arrayed and at the end of each semester every faculty member was provided with a "grade profile" of each class. Thus, a faculty member was able to determine whether the proportion of "A" caliber students was higher in a particular class than for the institution as a whole. Of course, this information was purely advisory but extremely useful.

How could an institution without endowment, relatively

small contribution income and a philosophy that did not have majority support at the time of its founding, survive in the spectrum of higher education? Many people assumed Roosevelt would not thrive for long—indeed its longevity borders on the miraculous. Nevertheless, there are multiple explanations, including the effects of the GI Bill, the urban location, and the appeal of cultural diversity. Much credit, however, also must go to a dedicated administration and a productive if underpaid faculty, teaching a fifteen semester-hour load and often additional hours for much less than proportionate compensation. Moreover, average class size in the early years hovered around 30 and did not decline until the impact of the Korean War, when it dropped to 26 in 1950. It was not unusual for a faculty member in business, the social sciences or the humanities to have 150 students enrolled in his or her five sections each semester.

In spite of this heavy teaching load, many faculty members were productive researchers. No one will ever convince me that lower teaching loads, although clearly desirable, assure greater productivity. While in the long run colleges would benefit from reducing the teaching load of those with proven research productivity (rather than granting across-the-board load reduction), the ability to do this depends on competition for faculty at any given period.

Acquisition of the Auditorium Building

Second in importance to the founding of Roosevelt College was the daring acquisition of the Auditorium Building during the 1946-47 academic year. It became evident soon after the College opened that it could not function in the inadequate building at the corner of Quincy and Wells. The Auditorium Building on Michigan and Congress, designed by Sullivan and Adler in the late 1880s, stood empty at the end of World War II and seemed doomed to demolition. Undoubtedly the only reason that the 500,000 square foot facility, with its all-masonry construction and huge granite footings, had not been demolished was the immense cost of doing so. The fact that such destruction would also have been barbaric would not have saved the building in a period predating the now prevalent landmark preservation attitudes in Chicago.

Ferdinand Peck, who had commissioned Louis Sullivan and Dankmar Adler to design the Auditorium Building, had based his planning on a multiple purpose building concept decades ahead of its time. The developers had hoped that by combining an opera house for Chicago with a hotel and an office building, the building's financial integrity would be assured. The plan was that the income from the Wabash Avenue side office building and from the hotel that encompassed the Michigan Avenue and much of the Congress Street frontage would help finance the physical maintenance of the Auditorium Theatre, located in the bowels of this huge building and without any of its own exterior walls. The building's magnificent design and its ingenious engineering (floating foundation, hydraulic power and primitive air cooling) are adequately described in other publications. Let it suffice to say that the functional concepts underlying Sullivan and Adler's philosophy made possible an extremely flexible adaptability for this spectacular building.

Historically, the building had been the victim of several financial crises. The most serious one resulted from utilities executive Samuel Insull's decision to build the Civic Opera House as an improved facility for the Chicago Opera Company and as a monument to himself. With the removal of a resident opera company from the Auditorium Theatre and with newer hotels taking the place of the grand old Auditorium Hotel, the building seemed doomed by the time America entered into World War II. During the war, the theater was converted into the largest USO facility in the country and during this period was severely damaged internally. Theater seats were removed from the main floor and the space became a huge bowling emporium. What is now the Rudolph Ganz Recital Hall, previously a gem of a private dining room and later a Freemasons ceremonial hall, became an officers' dormitory. Stained glass was painted over to keep out the sunlight. Wood paneling was destroyed and other parts of the interior deteriorated from neglect.

Aside from the physical deterioration, serious financial problems had taken their toll. During the Depression, taxes went unpaid and building liens reached enormous amounts. Moreover, the ownership structure of the building had become rather complex. When Roosevelt University decided to negotiate the building's acquisition, it was initially impossible to obtain the north twenty feet of the building, which included the heating plant and were owned by a syndicate of individuals represented by attorney Abraham Teitelbaum. Before we opened in the fall of 1947, these owners strung chicken wire across the Michigan Avenue corridor, separating facilities to which we had gained title from those which were being priced at what seemed to be an excessive amount. Students decided that they were going to have a "Chicken Wire Party" in this as yet unoccupied building. In those days *Life* magazine ran a weekly feature entitled "'LIFE Goes to a Party," which one week brought national attention to our Chicken Wire Dance. Public support for our efforts to preserve and convert the Auditorium Building brought considerable pressure on Attorney Teitelbaum and his clients. They finally sold the small but critical portion of the building to us. The College had to assume the back taxes in addition to paying $1,400,000, of which $400,000 went to the Teitelbaum group. These political and legal negotiations were protracted and, fortunately, the College was assisted in the transaction by many good friends, including a prominent Board member, Judge William J. Campbell.

The acquisition of this building (in hindsight, a stroke of genius) was the subject of much future controversy, as are most major issues facing a democratic educational institution. The antagonists considered the building too large, too old and too burdened financially. As I look back on this six-month period, it seems to me miraculous, based on my later experience with construction and remodeling, that it was possible for Roosevelt to sell the 231 South Wells Street building (now the location of the Federal Reserve Bank Annex), remodel the Auditorium Building sufficiently for classes to meet, satisfy the fire department, move the laboratories and library and register students in the new facility in the fall of 1947.

It is with nostalgia that I recall the cleanup work done with the assistance of faculty and staff. In fact I treasure a picture of my wife and President Sparling's daughter, Mary Ann, sweeping the main stairway prior to the opening of the new facility. The College could not afford to buy new furnishings. Most of the chairs, desks and file cabinets were war surplus material. People were able to ignore the old used furnishings, however, because of the intrinsic beauty of the building and its magnificent location overlooking Grant Park and Lake Michigan.

Much of the move seems analogous to what the opening of the Oklahoma Territory must have been like early in the 20th Century. Administration and faculty members rushed in to stake their claims to offices in the old hotel portion of the building. Where else in the country could a faculty member have an office with a private bath? Only later could we gain additional space and eliminate plumbing headaches by removing some of these bathrooms. Once, about ten years later when a faculty member requested of Jerome Stone, the then Board Chairman to save his bathroom, the humorous response was, "We will try not to discommode you." Those of us who benefited from Michigan Avenue offices were fortunate because the administration had not yet developed a space allocation rationale. We decided much later that, whenever possible, faculty offices should be located on the Congress and Wabash sides, and that classrooms should have the priority of being in the less noisy and more beautiful areas of the building.

Since 1947, the building has been greatly improved internally and has become a magnificent home for Roosevelt University. Regrettably, some of the building's antique features could not be preserved. For example, the original elevators, hydraulic and manually operated, had beautiful ornamental cabs with ironwork doors. These disappeared mysteriously as did much of the stained glass, probably appropriated over the years by people working on the premises.

Roosevelt University Board Faces Policy Issues

Edwin Embree, the first Chairman of the Board, served until 1948, during the period of rapid growth described in the previous chapter. Embree was succeeded by Harold Ickes, long-time Secretary of the Interior, who, according to many reports, ran Board meetings between 1948 and 1950 like an old curmudgeon. Reportedly, he tolerated little discussion, moved through the agenda at great speed and endeared himself neither to the administration nor the faculty. In 1950 President Sparling convinced Leo Lerner, a leading liberal and publisher of the Lerner Newspapers, a chain of neighborhood publications, to take on the chairmanship. Lerner and his wife, Deena, became deeply involved with the University for a decade. Lerner's dedication was matched by strong opinions and a flair for boldly stating policy positions. As a result he engendered great loyalty from his friends and animosity from those who differed with his point of view.

During the Lerner years, two major policy issues confronted the University. The first was the merger of the Chicago Musical College into Roosevelt, which resulted in the official name change from "College" to "University." The second, which continued up to 1989, related to the future of the Auditorium Theatre.

Chicago Musical College was founded in 1867 by Florenz Ziegfeld, the elder, and since 1933 had been presided over by Rudolph Ganz, a world renowned composer, conductor and pianist—a man of great personal charm who was highly respected and beloved in the musical world. Although Ganz turned seventy-seven in 1952, he continued to teach piano for fifteen more years.

Roosevelt College had always had a music school presided over since its founding by Joseph Creanza, an able dean of mercurial personality. Creanza was determined to bring about the merger with Chicago Musical College, an institution with a glorious past and a mountain of financial difficulties.

The issue to be faced was similar to that frequently encountered in corporate mergers. Since music schools are not known as "profit centers," the University debate centered around the question of whether economies resulting from the merger would result in a less costly operation and bring about a lower deficit than existed in the two separate institutions.

President Sparling took one side and Dean of Faculties Leys and Business Vice President Lowell Huelster took the other. The argument in favor of the merger pertained to prestige and public relations versus fiscal considerations. Sparling persuaded the Board to go ahead with the merger, although in-fighting continued for many years. It is fair to say that Chicago Musical College contributed to Roosevelt's prestige in the musical world, particularly because of Rudolph Ganz and Mollie Margolies. And the one major financial asset of Chicago Musical College was its small building on East Van Buren Street, which has since been torn down. On the other hand, the Chicago Musical College has been a major deficit operation since the 1954 merger.

Fiscal success, of course, is not the only objective of a university. Indeed, certain sectors do not contribute to the bottom line. Medical schools, for example, are frequently a drain on an institution's resources but prestige and enhanced fund-raising opportunities, not to mention service to humanity, are meaningful offsetting factors. Chicago Musical College accomplished little fund raising as an independent institution and this did not change with the merger. In fact, for many years to come, the University constantly struggled with an increasing drain of funds from other University objectives in order to preserve the quality of this relatively large music school. On the positive side, however, the Chicago Musical College attracted talented faculty and students who contributed much to Roosevelt's and the city's cultural life. These benefits offset certain faculty bitterness regarding money that could have enhanced salary levels but was instead absorbed by Chicago Musical College.

A much more serious controversy was the split that developed among the Board, administration, and faculty over the restoration and operation of the once magnificent Auditorium Theatre owned by the University and "dark" since the end of

World War II. Throughout the '50s there had been occasional interest on the part of various organizations in the possible restoration of this 4,000-seat theater. At one point the National Broadcasting Company was interested in using it for national television programming. President Sparling felt strongly that the University should undertake the restoration, that a restored theater would be a major educational resource for the community, In fact, in the early '50s it was believed that thousands of people would come to hear great speakers debate world issues. Television, of course, changed all that. As much as Sparling favored the restoration, so Leo Lerner opposed it. They disagreed not on the desirability of the restoration, but rather on the University fiscal problems that would result. Opponents feared that administrative time raising funds for the academic program would be diverted to the theater.

Lerner tried to find a way of having the theater restored under independent auspices with some form of guaranteed income to the University, which was in desperate need of developmental funds. It is unclear from the record whether Lerner's plan was implemented, although conversations regarding an independent development structure did take place with Arnold Maremont, a highly regarded Chicago business leader and a former Board member.

Great bitterness about this issue lasted for years. The dispute came to a head in 1959, resulting in the one major crisis in the Board's history. When the compromise decision was finally reached, it was unacceptable to Lerner, to two other Board trustees—vice president for academic affairs, John Golay, and vice president for development Wells Burnette—and to Wayne A. R. Leys, graduate dean and former dean of faculties, all of whom resigned. There were three factions on the Board: those supporting Sparling, those supporting the Chairman of the Board, and a middle group that supported a compromise solution, authorizing Beatrice Spachner, a member of the Roosevelt Board, to develop the Auditorium Theatre Council, which would be a creature of the University but would have an independent board whose membership would overlap with the University's Board. This council was authorized to raise funds in the name of the Auditorium Theatre Council for restoration purposes only and would, subsequent to the restoration, be permitted to operate the theater, subject to control by the Roosevelt Board but not its administration. This compromise was designed to keep President Sparling from devoting time to the theater, something greatly feared by Board members, and to disallow fundraising in the University's name for a purpose that would divert funds from university operations to theater restoration.

As a former violinist and music lover, Beatrice Spachner was uniquely suited to this task. She had previously raised funds for the lovely recital hall restoration on the seventh floor, later named in honor of Rudolph Ganz. Mrs. Spachner's dedication to the objective of restoring the theater was total.

Fortunately for the University, the compromise did not result in the resignation of all of the antagonists to the restoration efforts. Board members who remained included Jerome Stone, later Chairman of the Board; Max Robert Schrayer, later Vice Chairman of the Board, and Harold Friedman. However, as with many compromises, the conflict left permanent wounds and resulted in difficulties for years to come.

Although Mrs. Spachner should be credited with superhuman fundraising efforts and the restoration of one of the most beautiful theaters in the world, she and her Council developed a desire for independence which made coordination with the University extremely difficult. Although the theater never produced any income for the University's operations and the Council had the benefits of rent-free use of the facilities and of certain auxiliary services from the University, Roosevelt was never appropriately credited. In fact, every effort was made to conceal the affiliation with Roosevelt.

From a public relations point of view, the resignation of Leo Lerner and other officers of the University was indeed a setback. Harland Allen, an economist and investment adviser, became Chairman of the Board in 1959, and made valiant efforts to heal the wounds which festered for thirty years. Through the leadership of my successor, Dr. Theodore Gross, the Auditorium Theatre Council became responsible to the President of the University, a change that Jim Sparling would have heartily approved.

6

The '60s—A Decade of Crisis At Roosevelt University

Fifteen years after its founding, Roosevelt University had reached a plateau. Enrollment was still growing but at a slower rate. A major shift had taken place from lower division enrollment to upper division and graduate enrollments with a concomitant increase in operating costs. Salary levels had risen and become more competitive. Alumni were beginning to move into positions of importance. Increasingly, however, the University was facing competition from ambitious public institutions, including the University of Illinois, which was on the verge of expanding from a two-year extension into a major four-year university.

I watched these developments from my vantage point as Chairman of the Finance Department and dean of the business school, a position I assumed in 1957. Since its early days, the University's acceptance in the business community had greatly improved—I like to think my relationship with business leaders contributed to this.

In the early '60s, Jim Sparling had to face some rather serious financial crises. The loss of Wells Burnette, vice president for development, as a result of the Auditorium controversy, and some rather inadequate personnel replacements in development hampered fundraising efforts. Although buoyant to the last, Sparling began to show the strains of his job. I served on the Board of Trustees as an elected faculty representative at the time and it became clear that Jim's disposition was becoming increasingly testy when challenged. This was particularly noticeable in his relationship with Harland Allen, who had become the Chairman after the Auditorium fiasco. Fiscal years 1962 through 1965 were deficit years for the University budget, much of the difficulty undoubtedly resulting from Budget Committee pressure to improve salaries.

Some faculty politicians took advantage of Sparling's tendency to respond to challenges affirmatively, as demonstrated by an interchange which occurred towards the end of our annual series of budget meetings (which often resembled collective bargaining sessions). Professor Bernard Greenberg, an elected faculty member of the Budget Committee, remarked, "Jim, with your great ability we can write up the fundraising budget safely." To which Sparling replied, "If all of you will put your shoulder to the wheel and bring in more students, we will make it," thus agreeing to an increase in the "goal."

I do not know and the record does not indicate whether there were any private confrontations between Sparling and Allen, but the tension became more obvious and Jim began to say things like, "You will not have this president to kick around much longer." I don't believe he really meant these things, but he repeatedly talked about retirement. In hindsight it is very clear that leverage obtained by a veiled threat of resignation is an extremely dangerous management tool. At one particular Board meeting, when Jim talked about retirement, Allen (with a suddenness that signaled premeditation) said, "Jim, do you really mean this?" Sparling, completely incapable of denying that he meant what he said, responded in the affirmative. Whereupon Allen requested approval for the appointment of a search committee to recommend a successor to the founding president.

Lyle Spencer became chairman of the nominating committee and it was formed with Board, faculty and community representation. As a faculty Board member I was asked to serve as secretary of the committee. This 1963 search preceded current affirmative action advertising practices and relied heavily on personal recommendations via the "old boy" network. Spencer, who headed Science Research Associates, and was a business-man-scholar, developed his own little brain trust to assist in the search. His personal advisers were Charles Dollard, formerly head of the Carnegie Foundation, and Ralph Tyler, a highly respected educator. A long list of possible candidates was assembled and a screening process began. My role was to arrange logistics for the visiting candidates, but this extremely difficult because of a conflict between my loyalty to Sparling and my pledge of confidentiality to the committee. Frequently, I found myself on the spot when Jim wanted a status report. I explained this to Sparling and offered to resign. He did not want me to do this. I then explained the difficulty to Spencer and asked him to keep Sparling informed. He icily responded, "Leave it to me to keep Jim's paranoia under control."

The search was a difficult one. As usual, there were many frivolous applications to screen out. After several months a short list of top candidates was developed. Spencer insisted that incognito visits be made to the campuses of the finalists, which subjected the list to further pruning. Spencer also applied extremely high standards to candidates' "personal habits." In fact, two individuals, who later assumed positions of major importance on the national scene, were eliminated on the basis of "moral" considerations. And the first two candidates to whom the position was offered turned us down. (One later became a vice president at Florida State, president of the University of Rhode Island, and chancellor of the University of Wisconsin at Milwaukee. The second candidate later became president of Northern Illinois University.)

Roosevelt's major obstacles in securing Sparling's successor resulted from the University's accumulated deficit, the thrust of strong public sector competition and the heavy dependence on tuition. Indeed, observers felt that Roosevelt would not survive the strong University of Illinois presence.

The committee turned its attention to a promising young candidate, Robert J. Pitchell, who had served as administrative assistant to Senator Birch Bayh in Washington, D.C., and was associate director of the Institute of Public Administration at Indiana University, where he was also a member of the political science department. Pitchell had among his recommendations excellent letters of support from Herman Wells, the much respected President of Indiana University and from Senator Bayh.

He was considered to be politically liberal and someone in consonance with Roosevelt's traditions. He made an excellent impression in his interviews and during the campus visits. He was highly articulate, prematurely gray and fit the folkloric image of a college president. Pitchell was appointed at the Board of Trustees meeting, on October 24, 1963. There was great hope that the University would get a new thrust and earn improved community acceptance under his leadership. Rarely have such high hopes for a new president in an American university been dashed so quickly.

The Failed Presidency

In spite of Pitchell's intelligence and good academic record, his lack of experience in a major administrative responsibility quickly became evident. It serves no useful purpose to go into details regarding personality, but there are lessons to be learned from the experience of 1964, most importantly that every university has a "culture" of its own and that any attempt at radical change in a short time is most likely doomed to failure.

Pitchell arrived on campus with two assistants, one of whom bragged about being the president's hatchet man. A new faculty manual was prepared, borrowing heavily from that of Indiana University without full awareness of the differences between Bloomington and Chicago. Moreover, there was a preoccupation with the perquisites of office, including the president's apartment and the rebuilding of the president's office. (Symbolic of the latter was Pitchell's decision to knock out part of a wall in order to replace a one-door entry to the president's office with double doors.)

The second lesson derives from personnel and policy matters. Roosevelt was built on a model of faculty democracy that was not only unusual for that time, but remains so to this day. Although I have only circumstantial evidence, I believe that Pitchell was encouraged to make major changes by Spencer who had taken over the Board chairmanship in 1963. The proposed changes were inspired primarily by a Board-commissioned study conducted by Cresap, McCormick and Paget. Their report recommended removal of faculty from the Board, the abolishing of votes of confidence, and the discontinuation of the faculty budget committee. Unfortunately, Pitchell did not have the diplomatic skills necessary to bring about smooth change. Fears created by these recommendations and the disaffection on the part of the deans soon made it almost impossible for Pitchell to function.

I believe, however, that Pitchell could have survived in office even replacing all the deans, had it not been for serious disagreements on financial matters resulting in his unfortunate dismissal of the vice president for business and finance, an able administrator of great integrity. Within a matter of approximately six months, the Board came to the reluctant conclusion that the new president was not able to cope with the "rebellion" of the administrators (who demanded and received a hearing by a committee of the Board) and at the same time solve the serious financial difficulties the University faced.

In early fall of 1964 the Board decided to separate the internal and external responsibilities of University administration. The internal functions were to be performed by an elected chairman of the Administrative Council. Internal policies were to be submitted to the president for concurrence. In case of disagreement, the Board was to function as arbiter. Pitchell was told to concentrate exclusively on fundraising and other external activities. It is not clear what the Board hoped to accomplish by this restructuring, but I suspect that they would not have been unhappy if Pitchell had refused to accept it and had submitted his resignation. Clearly, the change must have been demeaning to Pitchell, who increasingly showed the stress of his responsibilities.

I was elected by my colleagues in the administration as chairman of the Administrative Council, which consisted of the vice presidents, the deans and the librarian. While I was pleased by their confidence, I was also intimidated by the difficult task of maintaining rapport with Pitchell, representing the interests of the other administrators and faculty, and serving as a loyal Board member. I was indeed walking a tightrope.

During the latter part of 1964 the relationship between the president and the administration on the one hand and the president and the Board of Trustees on the other deteriorated beyond repair. In my judgment, Lyle Spencer was eager to get a change of administration without undue publicity, a tactic entirely in keeping with Spencer's self-image as a smooth administrator. However, one of the deans, although agreeing generally with other administrators, decided to wage his own "campaign" against the president. He first prepared a psychological profile of Pitchell, which he sent to the Chairman of the Board, who was justifiably appalled by what he considered an unprofessional act. Second, a "leak" ostensibly originated from this dean to the student newspaper, *The Torch,* suggesting Pitchell had been fired. The subsequent student newspaper headline resulted in an irate reaction from the Board Chairman, who felt that a resignation request would make the Board look scooped by the newspaper.

By December of 1964, leading Board members had decided that a presidential change was essential. The year had been a financial disaster and all but one or two deans were prepared to resign if no changes were forthcoming. Matters came to a head in the last week of December. Pitchell, reportedly in Arizona, could not be reached by Spencer, but the Board decided to request his resignation as of December 31, 1964.

During that week Spencer asked me to assume the acting presidency with the clear understanding that I would remain Dean of the College of Business Administration and that I would not seek the permanent presidential appointment. He pointed out, however, that I was to function as if I were the permanent president and not simply a caretaker. I felt deeply honored by the trust and frankly somewhat afraid of the immense responsibility of reversing a deteriorating situation in faculty morale and financial stability.

On December 31, the Board called a press conference at the Mid-America Club to announce both my appointment as Acting

President and the reactivation of the search committee. My marching orders from the Board were clear: restore the fiscal integrity of the University, improve its image, and create stability—a tall order indeed. I accepted this responsibility because it was a great honor and because I knew that I would have faculty and administration support.

The Acting Presidency

In the literature on higher education administration little if any attention is paid to the difficulties encountered by those serving in an acting capacity. While an acting president has the responsibility and authority to function as president, his or her role is similar to that of a "lame duck." On the assumption that I would in due course return to my deanship, I also had to appoint an acting dean for the College of Business Administration. Interim period uncertainties made recruiting difficult.

Further problems arose because our first efforts at transition had failed and had not helped our public image. I was confronted with an accumulated deficit in excess of $800,000, a precarious fiscal fact given an annual budget of $4.8 million. One of my first undertakings was to negotiate a line of credit at the American National Bank in order to meet the payroll punctually.

Having to cut budgets immediately after taking over the stewardship is usually not the path to popularity. I was extremely fortunate curing this budget crisis to have many friends on the faculty and total support of the administration and the faculty budget committee. Budget-making at Roosevelt had for years been an unusually democratic process, with three administrators and three faculty members going through the entire budget line by line. While cumbersome, in times of retrenchment it was extremely helpful in getting cooperation.

In addition to the leadership and fiscal crises, the late '60s became a major enrollment challenge. To prepare for the ramifications of the post-war baby boom, the State of Illinois implemented a large expansion in the public sector to higher education. Besides the development of a major campus of the University of Illinois, two former teachers colleges had become broadly based urban institutions of higher education—Northeastern Illinois University and Chicago State University. Moreover, Governors State University in the southern suburbs and Northern Illinois University began to draw students from the Chicago area. Roosevelt was confronting a major marketing dilemma—we needed a new niche to justify our raison d'etre. It became very clear that a policy of nondiscriminatory education was insufficient. My colleagues and I were convinced that we had to become educationally experimental and progressive and we decided to focus on degree programs for adults, become a mecca for transfer students from the rapidly expanding community college system and develop special programs for culturally deprived youngsters of ability.

Furthermore, an upgrading of our physical facilities was absolutely essential in order to succeed in this increasingly competitive environment. We would take advantage of federal legislation and through a combination of private and government dollars build a ten-story building in the light and air court, tear down a neighboring loft building which has been acquired during the Sparling administration, construct a combined student union and dormitory building and renovate the unused tower on top of the Auditorium Building in addition to modernizing and air-conditioning a substantial portion of the Auditorium Buidling itself.

The "acting" administration was successful in initiating new academic thrusts, construction plans and fiscal efforts. During fiscal year 1966 the accumulated deficit was reduced by almost fifty percent and a campaign for $7.5 million was launched, a substantial proportion of which was raised from private sources. Fortunately, the Board of Trustees rallied in support of the institution at a difficult time. During this period the University was also able to initiate meaningful programs that provided evidence of our traditional concern for societal needs: a Peace Corps training program and an Upward Bound program to enable disadvantaged high school students to make the transition from secondary to higher education were launched. We also began our involvement in the training of Head Start teachers and participated in a national teacher corps consortium. Possibly the most significant curricular development started with a tiny seed grant of less than $5,000 from the Sears Foundation, which enabled us to develop our Bachelor of General Studies program, thanks in large part to the imaginative contributions of Professor (and later Dean) Lucy Ann Marx who, in turn, was greatly influenced by the pace-setting work of Professor Cyril Houle of the University of Chicago.

I would be remiss if I did not say a few words about the racial and religious discrimination of the '60s. Roosevelt was a pioneer in the field of nondiscrimination in higher education. And while we have come a long way in this country since World War II when segregation was the rule rather than the exception, even as late as the 1960s Jewish university presidents were a rarity and black administrators outside the Negro colleges were very few indeed.

Discrimination against Jews exists primarily in the social sphere and the important club life of America. When I became acting president Lyle Spencer suggested that I join an appropriate club and thought that the University Club of Chicago would be the most suitable. I told him that my being Jewish might create a problem there. Lyle put his arm around me and said, "Now, Rolf, don't you start out with a chip on your shoulder." I assured him that this was not at all the case and that I would be delighted to accept a membership if he could arrange it. Weeks later I learned that after a great deal of correspondence regarding my membership Spencer had concluded that the membership was not worth the trouble. I had no doubt that the religious issue was the stumbling block.

About two years later our then vice president for development, Wendell Arnold, again raised the question of club membership. He felt that it was inappropriate for all social entertaining on behalf of a nonsectarian university to take place at the Jewish Standard Club. I had already decided that I would make no effort to reapply to the University Club and that I would join only if invited. It is to the credit of Arnold and one of the trustees of the

University, Edgar Peske, who energetically pursued the matter, that the chairman of the membership committee of the University Club invited me to lunch to let me know that the Club did not discriminate against Jews. Clearly, times had changed. In fact, after my retirement, I had no difficulty turning over my membership to my Jewish successor.

Although throughout my twenty-four years in the presidency, I did not have to cope with any overt discrimination. I was always aware of the distinctions being made in the social arena. While I believe that America's leadership has become increasingly sensitized to the feelings of minorities, rather than criticize the occasional lapses, we have to applaud the tremendous progress made in race relations during the last thirty-five years.

Although I truly was not seeking the permanent appointment when I accepted the acting presidency, I would be less than honest if I did not admit that after a few months in office, I began to enjoy the challenge. However, I felt the odds were against my being selected and I was increasingly concerned about instability in the College of Business Administration without a permanent dean at its head. Although the Board of Trustees had interviewed at least two candidates, the search for a permanent president was not being pursued strenuously. It disturbed me greatly to learn that Professor Robert Runo, a faculty representative on the new search committee, had said that the faculty felt I was doing an adequate job and should be "kept in an acting position until somebody better comes along." This resulted in my telling Spencer that I wanted to return to my deanship in the fall of 1966. The Board was then forced to make a decision and in the summer of '66 I was asked to assume the presidency effective the 1966-67 academic year.

The Presidency

One of the bright periods of my life, a time when many things started to fall into place, came with my appointment to the presidency of Roosevelt in September 1966 and the events leading to my formal installation in April of 1967. Clearly Roosevelt was emerging from an extremely difficult period.

Budgets were being balanced again, enrollment was rising, and the University was finding more acceptance in the community.

In many ways, the early '60s was one of the best periods in the history of American higher education. Unfortunately, it was primarily because of the cold war and the "Sputnik" stimulus that governmental priorities shifted towards education. Government appropriations made it possible for Roosevelt to acquire scientific equipment and to launch our major construction program. While public policy at this time strengthened all of higher education, it clearly favored the expansion of the public sector. This would lead to major marketing problems for us in the '70s.

My inauguration as President took place in the newly restored Auditorium Theater in April 1967 (see chronology). I have attended many festive occasions, but I think even impartial observers would agree that this was one of the finest ceremonies ever held in Chicago. Hundreds of delegates marched through the arcaded Congress Parkway to enter the relit Auditorium. The filament bulbs over the proscenium arch glowed in a soft yellow light throughout the hall. Our student ushers were dressed in native garb of countries throughout the world, ranging from the flowing gowns of our Nigerian students to Indian saris. Among the participants were Nobel Laureate George Beadle, president of the University of Chicago; Mayor Richard J. Daley; my mentor, Professor Walter Weisskopf; Father John Cortelyou, president of DePaul University; Edward J. Sparling, the founding president of Roosevelt University; and Rabbi David Polish.

The events of the inaugural week were coordinated by my friend and one of the major pillars of Roosevelt's early years, Dr. Otto Wirth. An entire week filled with lectures and musical performances contributed to a renewed morale among faculty, students and friends of the University. Clearly dreams do come true and I only wished that my father, who succumbed to a heart attack in 1959, could have been present on this occasion. Only in America, it seems to me, is it possible for an immigrant with a minority group background and without substantial financial resources to be rewarded this way. Of course, many factors, including luck, are involved in achieving career goals. But in addition to luck, ability and hard work, a good family life plays an enormous part in contributing to one's success. Without the love and encouragement of my parents and the loyal support of my wife, I would never have reached this point in my career.

My first major task was to put in place an administration which would have the confidence not only of myself but of the faculty and the Board of Trustees. I was fortunate to be able to appoint, within a short period, my top administrators. Dr. Otto Wirth as vice president for academic affairs; Mr. David Kleinerman as vice president for business and finance; Dr. Lawrence Silverman as vice president for student services; Wendell Arnold as vice president for development; and Dr. Daniel Perlman, first assistant to the president and later as vice president for administrative services. This talented administrative cabinet had much to do with my success for the balance of the '60s and for much of the '70s. Wirth served until August 31, 1974, and was in many ways a father figure to many on the faculty. Kleinerman performed the important and difficult fiscal functions without creating antagonism. Silverman tackled marketing problems with great imagination and was instrumental in developing our suburban thrust. Arnold brought immense fundraising skills and became an adviser without parallel for two decades of my administration. Perlman, who moved on to the presidency of Suffolk University and later to Webster University, was a most creative team member in numerous governmental grants. Obviously, there were many others who played crucial roles during my tenure. Not all of these can be named in this short history but mention must be made of Harold Bland, who served, subsequent to David Kleinerman, for a long period in the business vice presidency, and Dominic Martia, who succeeded Lawrence Silverman after having served earlier as assistant to the president.

Chicago Daily News, October 31, 1966

Roosevelt's President Weil

Friends of Roosevelt University—and these should include all who see the importance of keeping opportunity for higher education open to all qualified persons—will wish Dr. Rolf A. Weil and the university the best of luck as he becomes Roosevelt's third president.

Some other colleges and universities are just now seeking ways to open their doors to students on the strict basis of ability and seriousness of purpose, which it was founded to do and has done since its beginning in 1945.

No selection of a university president is likely to please everybody—particularly

not at Roosevelt, with its tradition of vigorous dissent (sometimes, indeed, for the sake of dissent). But Weil and the university know each other thoroughly. Dr. Weil joined the faculty 20 years ago, and has been dean of the College of Business Administration and acting president.

Under his leadership and that of the board of trustees, whose president is Lyle M. Spencer, the university can be counted on to pursue ways by which not only Roosevelt but also other private colleges and universities may survive and thrive in a time of brutal competition with publicly supported institutions. Their facilities are needed to the full.

CHICAGO TRIBUNE, MONDAY, APRIL 17, 1967

Roosevelt U. Installs Dr. Weil

Dr. Rolf A. Weil was inaugurated as president of Roosevelt university yesterday afternoon in the university's Auditorium theater.

Mayor Daley congratulated Dr. Weil on behalf of the city, as did University of Chicago Chancellor George Beadle for the academic community.

The occasion also marked the school's 22nd anniversary and the reopening of the recently restored theater.

Pageantry Prevails

Pageantry prevailed as a procession of 500 representatives of colleges, universities, and academic societies thruout the nation marched in their caps and gowns from the university's Michigan avenue entrance around the corner to the theater. The somber tones of the educator's robes were brightened by gaily colored scarves.

In his inaugural address, Weil emphasized the interdependence of education and freedom. He indicated the role of today's colleges and universities is to educate the citizen to enable him to participate fully as a member of a free society.

"But education for freedom requires freedom for education," he asserted.

He called for competition among public and private schools and noted the need for federal and state aid to both to permit an accurate comparison of their worth.

Weil also urged more participation by the university in community affairs.

"The scholar must not be confined to his ivory tower," he said.

Comments on Projects

In a reference to student protests, Weil said a free uni-

versity must allow free speech and peaceful demonstrations. But he warned that they could not be permitted to disrupt educational and administrative functions.

He said some elements in protest movements have attempted to "make the university into a political tool."

Also speaking in the ceremonies were Dr. Edward J. Sparling, founder and president emeritus of Roosevelt; Otto Worth, dean of the faculty; Carmon Dunigan, student body president; Jerome Robbins, past president of the alumni association; and Lyle M. Spencer, board of trustees chairman, who installed Weil as president.

Weil, who joined Roosevelt's faculty in 1946, became acting president in December, 1964, and was elected president last October.

69

400 Scholars To Participate In Roosevelt U. Inaugural Events

An academic procession of 400 scholars and representatives of colleges, universities and learning societies form across the nation will march from the Michigan ave. entrance of Roosevelt University around the corner to Congress st. and into the newly restored Auditorium Theater where Dr. Rolf A. Weil will be inaugurated as third president of Roosevelt University on Sunday, April 6, 2:30 p.m.

Following greetings by Dr. George Beadle, chancellor, Richard George Beadle, chancellor, University of Chicago, for the academic community, and Mayor Richard J. Daley, for the city, the new president will be installed by Lyle M. Spencer, chairman of the board of trustees of Roosevelt University.

Rabbi David Polish, Beth EmetSynagogue, Evanston, will offer the invocation. The benediction will be given by the Very Reverend John R. Cortelyou, C. M., president, De Paul University.

Members of the University who will speak include Dr. Edward J. Sparling, founder and first president; Dr. Otto Worth, dean of facilities; Dr. Walter Weisskopf, faculty member; Carmon Dunigan, president of the student body, and Jerome Robbins, past president of the alumni association.

The Roosevelt University Chorus and Concert Choir conducted by Dr. David Larson, will provide choral music.

Following the ceremony, President and Mrs. Weil will receive friends and guests of the university in the second floor halls.

A black tie dinner, given by Board Chairman Lyle Spencer and Mrs. Spencer in honor of President and Mrs. Weil will receive President and Mrs. Weil, is scheduled for 8 p.m. at the Pick-Congress Hotel. In another part of the hotel members of the Edward J. Sparling Society of the university will sponsor a banquet.

*Edward J. Sparling—
President 1945-63. The
founder of Roosevelt
College had courage and
charisma.*

*Jim Sparling, with students'
commemorative scroll
honoring founders, speaks
with Marshall Field III and
Harold Ickes, Roosevelt
College's second Board
Chairman.*

*An early faculty meeting
at 231 South Wells Street
in Chicago. Idealism
prevailed.*

The Auditorium Theatre was saved from demolition. This picture of the Weil inauguration was the first event in restored theatre in 1967.

"Education for Freedom and Freedom for Education" was the topic of Rolf A. Weil's inaugural address.

Nobel Laureate George Beadle, President of the University of Chicago, brought greetings from the academic community to Roosevelt University's President Weil and Board Chairman, Lyle M. Spencer.

Herman Crown Center groundbreaking in 1970 was a major civic event in Chicago. Barry Crown, Chairman Jerome Stone, Mayor Richard J. Daley, President Weil and Colonel Henry Crown participated.

Benefactor Alyce DeCosta joins President Weil and Chairman Stone for the dedication of the Walter E. Heller Center in May 1943.

Harold Washington, Class of '49, Mayor of Chicago, 1983-87, brought honor and support to his alma mater.

Leni Weil was an active participant providing encouragement and support in Roosevelt University over four decades.

Board Chairman Alan Anixter greets President Weil at retirement dinner in 1988.

Theodore Gross is inaugurated in 1989 as Weil's successor and promises to build for the future.

7

Higher Education at the Ramparts

We had hardly begun to launch our construction program and our new adult education academic thrust when American higher education was confronted with the greatest student upheaval in U.S. history. What started with the free speech movement in San Francisco in the mid-'60s engulfed all of higher education and resulted in a major disruption of the American campus. Roosevelt University was not spared and the years 1967, 1968, and 1969 tested both our belief in freedom and our sanity.

The student unrest not only challenged leadership but produced in me a disillusionment with what had normally been considered campus "liberalism." The late '60s were a dangerous period for the American body politic—after this period ran its course it is reassuring to know that we returned to a greater degree of sanity in academe.

Unquestionably, our involvement in Vietnam was a major underlying cause for the malaise. This is not the place to debate the question of whether we should or should not have been embroiled in Southeast Asia. But it is certainly clear that a war cannot be fought successfully unless the government has made a firm decision to go all out not only militarily but also in its psychological preparation of society for such an effort and for a consensus of support. Our failure on both counts undoubtedly contributed to what occurred at American universities. In the true Roosevelt tradition, I was firmly committed to providing a forum hospitable to the airing of all views. There were no limitations on the distribution of literature or on the holding of open meetings. In no way, therefore, was the situation at Roosevelt comparable to that at the University of California in 1964. However, it became eminently clear that whatever happened on major campuses would be parrotted at Roosevelt. The same phrases such as "non-negotiable demands," "escalation," "exploitation of physical plant and cafeteria workers," "educational relevance," etc. emerged repeatedly. Ironically, janitors at Roosevelt, called members of an oppressed class, were unionized and not down-trodden members of the proletariat. The sociopolitical soil was fertile for revolt and it required only the catalyst of a small number of *agents provocateurs* to inflame feelings ranging from honest concerns about justice, peace and openness to political opportunism and radical nihilism.

Although the issues which provoked action each spring varied, the methods remained the same in '67, '68 and '69. Invariably protests started with oratory, followed by "non-nego-tiable demands" known to be unacceptable to the administration. Subsequently, pressure techniques and threats were used and finally a sit-in would either end with a negotiated settlement or fizzle as the semester drew to a close. While a majority of the students, staff or faculty were not involved in these events, the minority of activists controlled the agenda and the dynamics in each situation.

In 1967 we were confronted with what was known as the "ranking" issue. One of the most unfortunate policy decisions of the federal government during the Vietnam War was the exemp-tion from the military draft of male students who were academi-cally in the upper half of their class. This highly discriminatory policy in essence provided a draft exemption for most people in the middle and upper economic strata. Therefore, as we know, a much higher proportion of poor and minorities were drafted. The policy also created guilt feelings among women and exempted males and imposed on the academic community a most unfair burden. Institutional and departmental differences in academic requirements resulted in interference with students choices of majors as well as their selection of academic institutions. The academic community was overwhelmingly opposed to ranking and I joined many other university presidents in appealing to the government to change the policy.

In the spring of 1967 Roosevelt students demanded that the administration stop ranking. The administration made it clear in numerous pronouncements that we were opposed to the policy, but that the alternative of nonranking would subject all of our male students to the draft and would, in fact, destroy the institution through declining enrollment. The radicals on campus considered this reasoning unacceptable and threats led eventually to a sit-in. The hypocrisy of the radical leadership became eminently clear when the Dean of Students discovered that some of the student leaders had themselves requested to be ranked.

One of the major tactical issues confronting the administration was whether students should be permitted to sit-in after night closing hours. On some campuses, such all-night sit-ins were permitted in a specific building, such as an administrative facility. Because Roosevelt had only one main building it could not risk the occupation of its educational facility and the disruption of its academic program. The Administrative Council, therefore, decided that sit-ins would be permitted in specific areas but no interference with University operation would be tolerated and the building would be cleared of occupants at 10:30 p.m. This policy held much greater significance during the 1968 student revolt, but the principle was established in '67 and was immediately attacked by the leftists and their sympathizers.

The concept of an academic institution as a sanctuary for dissent was presented as if disruption were a freedom guaranteed by some mythical bill of rights. I have never been able to understand the double standard so commonly accepted by many liberal faculty members who condemn terror tactics by fascists but who consistently plead for sympathy and understanding for those with whose policies they agree regardless of their tactics.

The 1967 ranking controversy ended with the spring term. Although the issue did not reappear in the fall semester, a formal policy statement on "Freedom of Expression" was issued in November, 1967 (see pp. 83), wherein Roosevelt reaffirmed its continued support for the basic concepts of academic freedom, including such tactics as demonstrations, petitions, sit-ins, etc. The University also allied itself with the A.A.U.P. (Association of American University Professors) statement of December 1965, which stated that students should be "free to educate themselves by any orderly means which do not disrupt the regular and essential operation of the university." (A.A.U.P. *Bulletin,* December, 1965, pp. 447-49)

The unrest of 1967 pales in comparison with the upheaval that began in March of 1968, a year of crisis in U.S. foreign policy relating to the tragic events in Vietnam. Just as the country was severely divided on the Johnson administration policies, so were faculty and students divided on the role of the University. We hoped that these differences would be rationally discussed on campus. While no one expected that foreign policy issues could be resolved within the academic walls, one hoped that enlightened discussion would lead to legitimate activism in the political arena in spite of frustrations.

However, dissent took an ugly turn on campuses throughout the country from the University of California at Berkeley to Columbia University in New York. Events at Roosevelt paralleled the national pattern. What became an issue that drew the national spotlight to our relatively small university was the presence on campus of historian Dr. Staughton Lynd, whose views and activism had been on national view for some time.

It is important to summarize what led to the Staughton Lynd controversy, which rocked the Roosevelt community to its very foundation. Lynd is the adopted son of the famous husband and wife team of sociologists whose book, *Middletown,* became famous in the '30s. I did not think that Lynd was a communist, as has sometimes been suggested. I believe he would have described himself as a pacifist Quaker. However, an analysis of his career suggests that he was not interested simply in a vigorous pronouncement of his views, but rather in a pattern of behavior that, in my judgment, was designed to lead to martyrdom. Lynd became a controversial faculty member at Yale, where he was denied tenure. He repeatedly accused institutions of denying him academic freedom, an accusation which some of his most liberal colleagues considered unjustified. The fact that tenure denial at Yale was subsequent to Lynd's unauthorized travel to North

Vietnam is certainly not proof that Yale violated academic freedom. Lynd arrived in Chicago in 1968 to accept a full-time appointment at Chicago State University, but subsequent legal involvements resulted in a separation from Chicago State. He also applied for a position at the University of Chicago, although prior to academic appointment consideration he reportedly made accusations of lack of academic freedom there as well.

In his search for an academic home Lynd applied to Roosevelt's history department, where he had a part-time appointment. No one could deny that his academic credentials were excellent. Nevertheless, deviation from normal appointment procedures began almost immediately since Lynd's friends were obviously fearful that the Roosevelt administration would, as did other institutions, turn him down. Therefore, I was brought into the Lynd case prior to the formal appointment recommendation. What made the situation even more unusual was that prior to my decision not to appoint him, I received communications encouraging me to appoint him but also containing only slightly veiled threats of the consequences that would occur if I did not do so.

The Lynd application for a position at Roosevelt was the only instance that I know of where pressure was exerted on the administration in advance of the personnel consideration on the candidate's merits. Although the history department and the Dean of Arts and Sciences, George Watson, like Lynd a Quaker, recommended the appointment, the Dean of Faculties did not. I felt clearly that the appointment of a tenure-line faculty member, who was considered controversial not because of his views but because of his personality and his disruptive behavior pattern and on whose behalf unusual pressure was being exerted, would simply create an unnecessary problem for Roosevelt. Based on legal advice and for the protection of references, I indicated that the reason for denial was of an *ad hominem* nature, i.e., related to the individual's personality.

As had been threatened, all "hell" broke loose on March 29, 1968. The most offensive action by Lynd's faculty supporters was their accusation that the denial violated academic freedom and was based on Lynd's political views. The unfairness of this accusation should have been evident to all faculty members familiar with numerous previous Roosevelt appointments of people with widely differing views. A good institution should have a cross-section of academic orientations, but it is not necessary to appoint everyone with a controversial past simply to avoid the accusation of denial of academic freedom.

I am still puzzled as to why a significant number of faculty members became so aroused about the denial of appointment of a candidate who had been refused tenure by another institution, had a history of litigation against a neighboring institution and had been rejected for faculty appointment at a number of other institutions. The Lynd case demonstrated to me the vulnerability of a democratically managed institution. In such an institution the expectation is created that the administration's authority is severely limited and should never be asserted against the faculty will. This unrealistic expectation makes leadership highly vulnerable to charges of autocracy.

The American Association of University Professors, in cooperation with other umbrella organizations such as the Association of American Colleges, had agreed a number of years prior to the student unrest era on a policy statement which essentially says that in matters of appointment, tenure and promotion the wish of the faculty should be accommodated except in rare instances and for compelling reasons which should be stated in public. The Lynd case created no problem with regard to the first two conditions, but the matter of "publicly stated reasons" became a major issue. The administration of Roosevelt was literally "between a rock and a hard place" on this matter. Had we gone into detail on the matter of personality, we would have almost certainly been subjected to litigation and by categorizing the Lynd rejection on *ad hominem* grounds we were left vulnerable to the charge of being engaged in a conspiracy.

During the month of April 1968, various new organizations with high sounding names started a campaign of harassment against the Roosevelt administration. These included the Committee for Academic Freedom, Students for a Quality Education, the Chicago Committee to Defend the Bill of Rights, etc. In addition, the SDS (Students for a Democratic Society) became actively involved. Reportedly outsiders were brought in from as far away as California "to help stir things up." Information to this effect was provided to me by the FBI.

The administration spent endless hours negotiating in an effort to resolve the issue peacefully without surrender on the key issue, i.e., the denial of a three-year, full-time contract to Lynd. Actions escalated, leading to picketing of the University on May 6 and 7 and an attempt at a building takeover on Thursday, May 9. From the first week in May, the University was subjected to sit-ins, which, as mentioned earlier, were permitted in specified areas until 10:30 p.m. After this, students were requested to leave the premises or face arrest. The student revolt ringleaders arranged for daily votes as to who should be arrested. The dean of students informed me that these leaders always ducked out before the arrests were made. Unfortunately, a number of those arrested were decent but misled students. As the police had warned, an effort to take over key parts of the building and particularly the Development Office with its donor records took place on Thursday, May 9, when students invaded the Room 827 complex and chained the entryway. The chains were forcefully removed by the University and the students involved in this effort were arrested—sixteen were expelled.

In spite of the highly organized campaign on behalf of Staughton Lynd, which included faculty and students from other institutions, the majority of the faculty at Roosevelt either supported the administration or remained neutral. Votes of support for the administration came from the Alumni Association, the Senate Executive Committee and the Board of Trustees. The public media covered the events in both news stories and editorials (see chapter exhibits). The student newspaper, the *Roosevelt University Torch,* was at the time under leftist influence and supported the protesters. A very small number of faculty members actively encouraged the revolt and several of them resigned after having filed complaints against Roosevelt with the AAUP and the ACLU (American Civil Liberties Union). Investigations by both of these organizations subsequently cleared the University of all charges.

One cannot conclude the description of the 1968 Lynd affair without commenting on the fact that the black students, who made up a significant component of our student body, stayed almost completely out of this revolt, in spite of the fact that attempts were made to introduce racial issues into the controversy. One black student leader was overheard telling a white protest leader: "You do your thing and we will do ours."

The saddest part of the '68 experience was the fact that outsiders, including a well-known rabbi, sabotaged an agreement which had been reached by the University and the students by urging the protesters not to give in and to take the position that there would be no Roosevelt University without the appointment of Staughton Lynd. A *Chicago Sun-Times* editorial entitled "The University Destroyers" (see pp. 84) describes that lamentable outside involvement.

The climax of the '68 events took place at a mid-May meeting called exclusively for the purpose of discussing the Lynd matter. There were endless speeches in support of competing resolutions and it became increasingly evident that the Lynd supporters were prepared to filibuster until enough of their opponents had gone home. It was time to take a drastic step. I took the floor and stated that in my judgment all aspects of the issue had been debated, that I was going to leave the meeting and that I either needed a vote of support or would not be able to continue to function as president of the institution. After I left a vote was taken which supported but left wounds that took a considerable time to heal.

During this time I learned that left-wing groups believe that the behavior patterns of university administrators are primarily the result of pressures from corporate or wealthy individual contributors. At Roosevelt nothing could have been further from the truth. Indeed, the only threats to withhold contributions have come from ultra-liberals, most of whom were not significant supporters of the University. It hurt me deeply, however, when some of my old friends claimed that we took a strong stand, much applauded by the community, in order to curry favor with the establishment. Even though our stand had been favorably viewed in the business community, the fact that corporate support of Roosevelt University increased substantially in the '60s and '70s in my judgment had little to do with actions in the Staughton Lynd case.

As in 1967, the 1968 rites of spring ended with final semester examinations. There were a few humorous sidelights to the sad events of 1968. I was shocked when I saw a front-page newspaper picture of a mother handcuffed to her daughter. When I arrived at the office the mother called to tell me that all those who had been arrested were released at the police station after receiving a date for a court appearance. Mrs. X wanted to know what I thought of her. I told her that I had not thought much about it but that the occurrence saddened me. She said she was concerned that I might think poorly of her and she wanted to set the record straight. She had acted not out of agreement with the student radicals, but because, as a good Jewish mother, she felt a maternal need not to let her daughter be alone with all those bearded men.

Shortly after the events of '68 I received a phone call from a faculty wife, a member of the Daughters of the American Revolution, who told me that the DAR makes an annual award to an immigrant to the United States who exemplifies the spirit of the founding fathers. I had been voted this honor. I hesitated to accept it because I felt that it could again stir things up at the University. The good lady had read my mind and before I could comment she assured me that there would be no publicity. I should have known that something of this sort could not be kept confidential. Shortly after my accepting the DAR medal, the *Roosevelt University Torch* carried the headline "OUR DAR LING."

Although over sixty arrests were made in 1968, the University decided not to press the trespass charges. This was based on our belief that the purpose of the arrests was not to punish but to preserve the orderly processes of education. Our action in this matter resulted in an unpleasant confrontation between myself and Mr. Richard J. Elrod* of the State's Attorney's office, who was later seriously injured in a confrontation with Weathermen during the 1968 Democratic Convention. He was very upset by our unwillingness to press the charges and subtly threatened less cooperation in the future. I in turn tried to lecture him on the purpose of police work which, in my judgment, in the context of student unrest, was primarily to preserve order and should not concern itself with the judicial process.

The final student confrontation of the '60s occurred in the spring of '69 when the militant black students "did their thing." Unlike the '67 and '68 unrest, which was led by white students with practically no participation on the part of blacks and which had emphasized altruistic goals, the 1969 revolt had concrete monetary and power demands. Formally, the request was based on a demand for a new and expanded black studies program. Of course, these demands were being made nationally, but it is ironic that it became an issue at Roosevelt where Afro-American studies were a part of the curriculum since the very early days of the institution. Our program was on a very high level of scholarship and the teaching was done by such outstanding faculty members as the sociologist, St. Clair Drake; the anthropologist, Robert Roberts; and the linguist Lorenzo Turner. This program was small and had an interracial constituency. What the militant black students now wanted was a substantially funded undergraduate program which would include a lengthy list of such subjects as black politics and Swahili and above all funds for lecturers and for "assistants."

The overwhelming majority of our black students did not participate in the unrest but the situation became threatening, especially because of participation by the Black Panthers. Students were particularly harsh on faculty members with interracial

*Elrod later became Sheriff of Cook County and then a judge of the Circuit Court.

marriages. With regard to black faculty married to white women, the picket signs read, "He talks black but he sleeps white." In the reverse situation, the slogan was, "He is a throwback to slavery."

Just as at other institutions, we were presented with non-negotiable demands. The most intimidating moment was when the Black Panthers guarded every door to the presidential suite and were ready to invade my office. A number of my administrators were in my office when the invasion took place. We had barricaded the entrance with a sofa which provided little protection. The group stormed in, talking about "killing" us and about the execution list of the Panthers. Our hearts kept beating faster. A pen was pushed into my hand and I was asked to sign or else. I rushed to the phone on my desk to call for help but one of the students pushed me aside, tore the telephone out of the socket and threw it against the paneled wall.

Fortunately, someone outside the presidential suite had observed what was happening and had called the police. In the midst of this confrontation we heard the "guards" outside my office screaming "they have called the pigs" and the occupiers dispersed. Never had I been so happy to see the police. For several days thereafter I moved my office to the basement of the Congress Hotel and because of the threats, I had police protection for a few days. It soon became obvious however, that the police protection was unnecessary and I asked that it be discontinued. The students who had invaded my office were expelled from the University, again leading to my disillusionment with some of my "loyal" friends, who tried to tell me that I needed to learn the "new" language and that the word "kill" does not necessarily mean murder.

After rejecting some of the more ridiculous non-negotiable demands, we were successful in working out some compromises, which included the scheduling of certain courses, most of which never materialized for lack of enrollment. The best example of the curriculum nonsense was the request to add Swahili to our program. No one signed up for it, forcing us to cancel the offering. Although we expanded the Black Studies offerings at considerable cost to the University, it has become increasingly evident that black students are basically not interested in taking courses that do not contribute measurably to their upward mobility objectives.

I have always felt that for most of our students ethnic studies, including Black Studies, are most valuable when taken as enriching electives. The demand for Black Studies has declined and has become less of a political issue and more of a curricular interest. Black faculty members were extremely helpful to the administration during this period of unrest, although their moderating influence took place behind the scenes. Unfortunately, it has been said that many well-meaning and constructive black faculty and staff have felt intimidated for fear of being labeled "Uncle Toms" or worse.

Roosevelt University's Statement
on
FREEDOM of EXPRESSION

The era of the 1960's can best be characterized as one of ferment. Throughout our nation answers are being sought to new and complex questions regarding political, social or ethical principles. By its very nature, the modern university has become one of the major wellsprings of action which focuses on the search for answers to these questions.

For this quest of knowledge to continue it is necessary that all members of the university community be assured that their freedoms of speech and inquiry not be abrogated by the actions of others within this community. The "freedom even for the thought that we hate", which Justice Oliver Holmes pleaded for in the Rosika Schwimmer case must be jealously guarded if true academic freedom is to be maintained. It may be superfluous to remind all that in its short but vivid history Roosevelt University has supported and will continue to support these basic concepts of freedom.

Within recent history the exercise of these freedoms has been carried out in a variety of ways: teach-ins, petitions, and demonstrations being but a few examples. The expression of opinion by one or a number of individuals through all orderly procedures has been and will continue to be supported and encouraged by Roosevelt University.

In this regard we endorse and reaffirm as the policy of Roosevelt University the following statement of the American Association of University Professors:

> "Students and student organizations should be free to examine and discuss all questions of interest to them, and to express opinions publicly or privately. They should also be free to support causes by any orderly means which do not disrupt the regular and essential operation of the university." (51 AAUP Bulletin, pp. 447-449, Dec. 19654).

To make these principles effective in the life of the university we cannot condone any demonstration by an individual or group of individuals which restrain the freedom of expression or movement of others with whom they do not agree.

Rolf A. Weil, President - November 16, 1967

November 16, 1967

CHICAGO SUN-TIMES
EDITORIAL PAGE

The University Destroyers

A group of outside professors and other agitators have threatened to destroy Roosevelt University unless it hires the controversial history professor, Staughton Lynd. They say they are acting in the cause of academic freedom but surely the principle of academic freedom does not encompass the de̲____ of the temple in wh̲____ ___ must be prac̲____

T̲____
so̲____
N̲____

one from Northern Illinois University, said that it would urge teachers to refuse to accept jobs at Roosevelt unless Lynd was given a full-time appointment. One other member of the group said, "Either Lynd will be teaching at Roosevelt University or there will be no more Roosevelt University."

This outrageous threat calls for a counterattack by friends ___ alumni of Roosevelt Uni___ ___ we should hope, ___ ___ Roosevelt

itself who know better than anyone else the long record of respect for academic freedom built by Roosevelt University.

Lynd's case has been magnified out of all proportion to its importance. He was recommended for a permanent appointment by the Roosevelt history faculty. The appointment was vetoed by President Rolf A. Weil on the ground that Lynd's personality did not suit him to be permanently employed. Lynd is presently a part-time faculty member.

Lynd first ca__ ___ the atten- ___ he

CHICAGO DAILY NEWS
EDITORIAL

Tuesday, February 18, 1969

The limits of protest

University officials have found, to their sorrow, that there is no sure way to head off an assault by a determined group of radical students. Some of the most liberal institutions have been the hardest hit. Efforts to accommodate demands by either white radicals ___der' ___iations '

violence and in the virtual i__ ___ radicals, but left its mai__ of a cleanup ___ the h___ ___

the
___ite
s,
___

ARTICLE FROM
CHICAGO SUN-TIMES
Fri., Feb. 21, 1969

Storm Roosevelt Office, Threaten Weil

By James Casey
and Richard Foster

A group of 150 students, mostly black, burst in on Roosevelt University President Rolf A. Weil during a conference Thursday, demanding amnesty for expelled students and a black studies department.

Phones Torn Ou+

Emi'___ __nozz___ ___il's ___

stormed into his eighth-floor office about 11:30 a.m. as Weil was holding a scheduled administrative council meeting with about nine other university officials.

A university spokesman said that Weil was threatened during the meeting. Weil himself said later that the lives of several staff members were th___ ___ were te___ ___

and some equipment was destroyed, according to one university official. A fire hose on the eighth floor was pulled from its casing and water spilled down the elevator shaft and stairwell until it was turned off.

They burst into the meeting, Miss Panozzo related, ripped a telephone off the wall and made their dema___ Weil, sho___ occa___

84

STATEMENT OF THE STUDENTS WHO TOOK ROOM 827
ON 9 MAY 1968

Roosevelt University students are, at this moment, sitting quietly within the locked doors of the room containing the development office, The News and Broadcasting office, the Alumni Office and the Division of Continuing Education—that is, room 827.

These students will remain until President Weil is prepared to reverse his policy of political repression. For it is a political repression that has denied Staughton Lynd his job, a job which it is generally conceded, even by President Weil, Professor Lynd does with distinction and academic excellence.

The fact is, Staughton Lynd cannot teach here because he chose to step out of his ivory tower of academia and exercise his constitutional and moral right to involve himself in the great issues of our day—questions of life and death.

We have submitted to Pres. Weil a copy of the demands which students for a Quality Education have voted upon. They are:

1. Grant Staughton Lynd a 3-year, full-time teaching position.
2. Amnesty for all students confronting the administration on this issue.
3. No police on the University campus.
4. Open lines of communication between the president and students in the form of monthly meetings.
5. A constitutional provision eliminating administrative veto over faculty and student decisions.
6. Medical services for all persons on R.U. property, including cafeteria employees.

These are the demands which we are prepared to negotiate.

Let it be clearly understood that the students in Rm. 827 are prepared and intend to honor fully the student promise not to initiate either violence or destruction.

The students inside wish to express their complete solidarity with the many students who have given up valuable time to attend meetings, to picket, to boycott classes and to spend the night in Altgeld Hall. As fellow students, we know the depth of the sacrifice which you made.

We also wish to express our admiration for those students who were prepared to face prison records, suspensions and/or expulsion rather than compromise their beliefs, their morality, yes, their very dignity.

Finally, we ask for your support for we hold common demands, common commitments, common concerns—it is a common struggle.

CHICAGO TRIBUNE EDITORIAL
Monday, May 13, 1968

A PRESIDENT'S DUTY

President Rolf A. Weil of Roosevelt university continues resolute in refusing to abdicate the responsibilities of his office. Those include approval or disapproval of faculty appointments and use when needful of such sanctions as suspension and expulsion in defnese of order and respect for reguulations. Ray Page, superintendent of public instruction, has just said about insurrection at Southern Illinois university: "There are certain aspects of college and university administration that are absolutely nonnegotiable. We cannot surrender to the students the administrative responsibilities of our state colleges and universities." Nor should administrations of private schools surrender such responsibilities to stu-dents. It is their duty not to do so.

Staughton Lynd, the "new left" historian whose status at Roosevelt university is the occasion of current controversy there, argues that student participants in coercive sit-ins there should be immune from disciplinary action and from trespass charges. That fact alone provides ample confirmation of President Weil's judgment not to appoint him to the Roosevelt full time faculty. Student and faculty voices may and should be heard by administrators – in civil terms and thru appropriate channels. But in academic government executive responsibility must and therefore should be in the hands of the chief executive. President Weil is demonstrating what should be obvious to all.

STATEMENT BY PRESIDENT WEIL
July 19, 1968

I have previously indicated that I will not appoint Dr. Staughton Lynd to a full-time position on the faculty of Roosevelt University. Prior to this decision, the Dean of Arts & Sciences had offered a part-time appointment to Dr. Staughton Lynd for the next academic year. The University was prepared to issue a part-time contract on this basis. Dr. Lynd has now indicated that he will not accept such a contract.

The Dean of Arts & Sciences has now stated that he will not make a recommendation for the employment of Dr. Lynd in the future. As far as I am concerned, Dr. Lynd has now closed his case.

ROOSEVELT UNIVERSITY
Senate Executive Committee
Thursday, 9 May 1968

A meeting of the Senate Executive Committee, as led at the initiative of the Chairman (Paul Johnson), convened at 1:30 p.m. on Thursday, 9 May 1968. Present were: Professors Dorfman, Flora, Klemke, Bowers, and Snyder, President Weil, Dean Weeks, Dean Wirth, and Paul Johnson (chairman).

After general discussion, and consultation of the Roosevelt University Constitution, the following composite resolution was adopted by all those present.

1. The President of the University followed constitutional procedures in considering and deciding upon the appointment of Staughton Lynd, and did not exceed his constitutional powers in making a negative decision.

   The President in fact has the obligation to make the decision on appointments. As the Roosevelt University Constitution specifies (Article 1, Section 1), "All members of the Teaching Staff shall be appointed by the President after hearing the recommendations of the Dean of the College in which the appointment is sought and of the Chairman of the Department and its voting members."

2. Consultations between the President, the Dean of Faculties, and the Dean of the College of Arts and Sciences on the one hand, and the History Department members and other interested persons on the other hand, were frequent and lengthy; the administration repeatedly declared its willingness to discuss, and honored that declaration.

3. The constitutional procedure of Roosevelt University must be maintained in the interests of all.

   Regular, representative, democratic procedures exist at Roosevelt University.

   It is to these procedures that protesters and dissenters are urged to turn.

4. Recognizing that there is sincerity and honest conviction on both sides as to the issues in the Lynd controversy, we hold that the University must not submit its policy to dictation by pressure groups.

During the discussion of the above four resolutions, President Weil absented himself from the Committee deliberations.

Robert E. J. Snyder   Paul B. Johnson
Secretary   Chairman

Chicago Daily News, Friday, May 17, 1968

Lynd isn't worth it

Students everywhere seem impelled to tear up the campus these days, for whatever cause comes handy, and if there had been no Staughton Lynd the students at Roosevelt University doubtless could have found some other excuse. But because Lynd became the focus, and because the final power to hire and fire professors brooks no compromise, the record of the controversial professor bears examining.

It isn't a very pretty record, and the most pathetic feature of the whole unfortunate turmoil at Roosevelt may be that the cause really wasn't worth the struggle.

Controversy began boiling up around Lynd when he made an unauthorized trip to North Vietnam in 1965. That put him in the news, won him a crown of martyrdom and a reputation for sagacity with the New Left, and has been confusing the real issue ever since. For the real issue is not whether he is a Marxist, but whether he is a good historian and teacher. And this question keeps getting lost in the assumption that poor Staughton Lynd, a brilliant teacher, is being persecuted for his leftist views.

The evidence suggests that the assumption is false, for universities quite willing to examine radical views and hire radical professors shy away from Lynd. Many universities believe the campus is a proper place for the ferment and intellectual turmoil of Marxism. But they have had their chance at Lynd and turned him down. It seems clear that those universities who want a Marxist around can find a better one than Staughton Lynd.

The record shows that Lynd is peculiarly attracted to martyrdom, of which the Hanoi visit was only the most conspicuous example. And with each new turndown by another university he hoists the phony flag of "academic freedom" while he revels in his martyrdom. He did it at Yale, where the faculty regretfully voted against giving him tenure because they had found him so difficult to deal with. Lynd rushed over to the student newspaper and charged—falsely—that Yale had guaranteed him tenure and then reneged. It made quite a stir.

He did it again when the trustees overruled Chicago State College on hiring him last year, and kicked up such a fuss that he was put to work for a year on the understanding that he leave when the year was up. He has now charged that his academic freedom is being violated because Roosevelt University won't hire him.

It's hard to see what the beef is about unless academic freedom means that any professor is free to tear up any university that won't hire him. We don't believe that's what academic freedom is all about.

The fact that the fuss over Lynd reached the stage it did may speak poorly for the internal structure of Roosevelt University. Personnel and curriculum matters should be handled within the faculty and administration through a process that requires no overt exercise of final authority by the president or board of trustees. But when things do come to a showdown, there can be no question of where the final authority lies, and that authority was properly used at Roosevelt. Time alone will tell whether Lynd's new battle star of martyrdom has been gained at the expense of permanent damage to the university.

7359 S. Bennett Ave.
Chicago, Ill. 60649
July 15, 1968

Professor David Miller
Chairman, Department of History
Roosevelt University

Dear Dave:

Thank you for your patience in awaiting my decision about part-time work at Roosevelt next year. I have decided not to teach part-time at Roosevelt in 1968-69 (except at the Free School).

I want to make it clear that, of course, I still desire the full-time position which the history department recommended this year and which it has decided to recommend again next year.

The decision to decline part-time employment has been difficult, not least because I very much enjoyed teaching at Roosevelt in 1967-68. The reasons are as follows:

1. In offering me part-time employment, Dean Watson stated (in his letter to you of June 14): "I see no possibility that I could recommend a full-time appointment for the 1969-70 academic year; I hope the Department will not press for such an appointment." These remarks conceptualize part-time employment, not as a step which would leave the possibility of full-time employment open, but as a substitute for full-time employment. I conclude that attention can best be kept focussed on the central issue of a full-time appointment if I decline a part-time appointment. Dean Watson has assured me that his tentative decision not to support me for full-time work is not based on new evidence concerning my qualifications, but on concern for the stability of Roosevelt as an institution. I hope he will come to feel that Roosevelt as an institution can best grow if it returns to its traditional practice of hiring controversial teachers.

2. Two members of the department have resigned in protest against President Weil's decision. The Committee for Academic Freedom in Illinois has asked teachers to decline appointment at Roosevelt until the administration's policy changes. I believe that I can best support these actions by declining to do what Professor Bluestone and Haskett no longer feel able to do, and what SAFI has asked others not to begin.

Sincerely,

Staughton Lynd

cc: George Watson and John Lepp (Administration)
  Jack Roth and Donald Bluestone (history)
  James Bailey (Free School)
  Alfed Young (SAFI)
  Bertram Davis (AAUP)
  Jay Miller (Illinois ACLU)
  Bernard Farber (Roosevelt TORCH)
  Robert Bass (New University Conference)

The Staughton Lynd Appointment Issue

This is a statement for the record. Since I must be out of town at the time of the visit of the AAUP consultants, it is primarily but not exclusively for their information. I shall not attempt to review all the facts, since the record is quite full, but I shall comment on my own position and on my evaluation of the President's decision.

The issue of a full-time appointment for Staughton Lynd at Roosevelt University was first called to my attention in the fall of 1967 by the chairman of the History Department, Jack Roth. I was aware of the details of the controversy at Chicago State College and had signed a statement as a member of the Illinois Committee for Academic Freedom, which was supporting Lynd in that situation. I had known Lynd slightly from his attendance at 57th Street Meeting of Friends in the 1950's, when he was a graduate student at the University of Chicago, and came to know him much better during the current year, when he attended and participated actively in the Meeting for Worship and some of the committee work of the Friends Meeting. When I entertained the History Department for dinner in my home, I invited the Lynds and arranged for Staughton to sit near Rolf Weil. Because of the controversy surrounding Lynd, Roth anticipated that Weil might have doubts about an appointment and asked my advice on procedure. I suggested that he present the recommendation from the Department in the normal way after the first of the year, which he did.

I was aware that Lynd had been involved in an internal controversy over his tenure at Yale, and that during the fall of 1967 there had been some difficulties arising from an attempt to arrange an appointment for him at the University of Chicago, made by Marshall Hodgson, Chairman of the Committee on Social Thought, also a member of the Friends Meeting, and a close personal friend of mine. Both these controversies have since been spread on the record in the *Columbia Forum.* I took occasion to consult with Hodgson—a conversation which lasted for two and one-half hours—in order to be sure I understood what had occurred at the University of Chicago. I felt after this that I did understand quite thoroughly, because I know of no one more careful of the truth than Marshall Hodgson, whose recent death has been a very severe blow.

Hogdson's conclusion was that Lynd had behaved carelessly in checking factual information and irresponsibly in leaping into public utterance. However, he felt this was caused by lack of sophisticated understanding of the subtle processes underlying appointments at the University of Chicago and further, that Lynd had learned from the experience.

This kind of information seemed to me a valid element to weigh in the making of an initial appointment. However, in view of the very strong reasons in favor of appointing Lynd, and in view of my judgment that he is a person who would fit well on the Roosevelt University faculty, I made a favorable recommendation for his full-time appointment. Otto Wirth, Dean of Faculties, recommended against appointment, and Weil decided not to appoint.

The question is frequently raised how I could support Weil's decision on principle after he overruled my recommendation. I have supported him because I believe he made his decision on the basis of the right considerations, although he weighed them differently. The central issue as I see it is this: Is the prediction that a man will be a disruptive colleague, who makes unfair charges on the basis of inadequate information, sufficient ground for denying him initial appointment? This is a third kind of criterion, which is neither a question of academic competence, nor a question of political beliefs and utterances. It is therefore not covered by the statement of 1966, or any other statement I remember concerning academic freedom. Since the 1966 statement in effect proposes that initial appointments be considered to fall within the range of actions involving academic freedom, serious consideration should be given to this problem in revising the statement. While it is clear that this kind of judgment can be abused, it can hardly be rejected as a legitimate basics for decision.

I spent a considerable amount of time with Wirth and Weil trying to persuade them to accept my recommendation, and I participated in discussion with Roth and in the meeting with the History Department. The public reports issued by the Department, where they relate to conferences where I was present, seems to me to misrepresent Weil's position in order to create the impression that it was a "political" decision based on grounds violating academic freedom, when in my judgment it was not. I have been a colleague and friend of Rolf Weil for the past 22 years and an administrative associate for the past two. Having resigned one deanship, I can testify that I am now serving as a dean only because I could not refuse his insistence that the welfare of the university was involved. While my support of his position is therefore based on personal and institutional loyalty as well as on principle, this loyalty is not blind or dependent.

I have never known Weil to be dishonest in his statements; all my discussions with him and others in this matter lead me to the conclusion that he is being completely truthful in stating that personality rather than political grounds is the basis for his decision. However, he is temperamentally cautious and has a tendency to understate his position, so that those who are seeking grounds for disbelief can easily judge him to be evasive and equivocal. Much has been made of the fact that he referred, in discussions with Roth and the History faculty, to Lynd's political behavior, to fund-raising implications of an appointment, and to evaluations made by others writing about Lynd. In teaching administration, I tell my students that Watson's first law of decision-making is: Everyone always does everything from mixed motives. No one making a decision about Staughton Lynd will be able to expunge from his memory or his emotions what he believes he knows about Lynd's behavior. The question is what was the central ground of decision, rather than whether all other considerations were totally excluded.

It is very clear to me that the central ground of Weil's decision was an evaluation of Lynd as a prospective colleague who would participate in the internal policy-making processes of the University: who would have relations with department chairmen, deans, and the President; who would serve on committees and on the University Senate; and who, on the basis of information available, might make life exceedingly unpleasant for his colleagues and superiors. I weighed the evidence and judged that the risk was small and worth taking; Weil weighed it and judged the risk so great as to be unacceptable. I believe he made a mistake, but it was a mistake in the weighing of evidence and not a mistake in principle. I support him because of a firm conviction that the burden of making executive decisions inevitably entails making mistakes. The incidence of such mistakes is a measure of executive competence; in my opinion, Weil's incidence is very low. Where, as in this case, the mistake does not involve a violation of principle, it is not an appropriate basis for making emotional charges within the academic community.

To conclude the factual story: At the time of Weil's decision not to appoint, Roth told me that Lynd would be willing to accept a part-time appointment for the 1968-69 academic year of two courses per semester at the same rate ($1000 per course) he received during the 1967-68 year. I tried to persuade the members of the History Department not to make a public issue of the full-time appointment, in the belief that it would be possible to allay Weil's fears and have a full-time appointment approved for the academic year 1969-70. In this, of course, I did not succeed. Under my discretionary authority as Dean of the College of Arts and Sciences, it is my intention to issue a contract to Lynd for two courses for the 1968-69 fall semester, and unless the situation changes materially, to do the same for the spring. I have notified the incoming chairman of the History Department, David Miller, of this intention; I have also informed him that I do not feel I can recommend a full-time appointment for the academic year 1969-70 and that I hope the Department will not press for such an appointment.

George H. Watson
June 18, 1968

ROOSEVELT UNIVERSITY

May 6, 1968

TO: All Faculty and Students

FROM: The Administrative Council

RE: Demonstrations

Some students and faculty members of Roosevelt University are now engaged in picketing outside its doors and have stated their intention to engage in other activities directed toward a reconsideration of a personnel decision made in the case of Professor Staughton Lynd. The chief public statement they have issued has been a so-called "fact sheet" circulated by the History Department and an *ad hoc* faculty committee.

It seems important to clarify the position of the University and the procedures which have been followed in this case. The principles of academic freedom apply to all faculty members of Roosevelt University. These principles have been established over many decades by the excellent work of the American Association of University Professors. Roosevelt University has always affirmed and observed these principles in the fullest degree. They do not apply in the consideration of a candidate for appointment to a full-time position and therefore are not at issue in this case, although the critics of the University's action have been implying that they are.

The process of appointment of a full-time faculty member involves consideration by the members of the department, recommendations by the dean of the college and the dean of faculties, and decision by the president. This is the recognized procedure in institutions like Roosevelt which have a very large measure of faculty self-government. Those procedures were followed in this instance, and more extensive collection of information than is customary was made before the president decided this issue, because of the intensity of concern on the part both of those who supported and of those who opposed the appointment. In our present procedures there is no alternative way of making such a decision. The faculty through its representative process is always free to change its constitution and therefore to change such procedures, subject to approval by the Board of Trustees.

Since the decision was announced, the president has continued to consult at great length with the History Department, with representatives of the faculty and student committees and with individuals who expressed concern.

With regard to the actions which are now being taken to influence this decision, we should like to call attention to the statement issued by President Weil on November 16, 1967, stating the University's support of the freedom of students and faculty to express their opinions in a variety of legitimate ways. This does not include activities which "disrupt the regular and essential operation of the University". We have previously stated the limits of permissible activity; in fairness to those who wish to engage in legitimate protest, we do so again at this time:

> Students and faculty members are free to hold meetings and demonstrations which do not interfere with the regular conduct of classes and other University business.

> Demonstrators must leave offices when they are closed at the end of the University's working day and must leave the building when it is closed at the regular closing times of 10:30 p.m. on weekdays and 6 p.m. on Saturdays. No demonstrations will be permitted in inner working offices.

If these restrictions are observed there need be no difficult confrontations between the University and any demonstrators. Should such a confrontation be forced, we will, as in past instances, use the means that are necessary to maintain the operation of the institution to safeguard the academic freedom and the rights of other students and faculty members and to insure the security of University records and the safety of its building.

Roosevelt Prexy Speaks

Protests Justifiable— to a Point, Says Weil

BY PAT DALTON

Dr. Rolf A. Weil, president of Roosevelt university, is a man who knows a lot about student rebellions, both first-hand and academically.

He has been studying student outbursts since the first one began at the University of California in Berkeley in 1964. During the last week, he has been dealing with black student protesters on his own campus who claim the study program for blacks is inadequate.

There were no demonstrations at Roosevelt yesterday. A student faculty committee met last night and agreed on a plan to establish a black studies department.

The plan was formed by the Black Studies Curriculum committee. It calls for the Black Student association to draft a specific course of study and administrative operation.

It would have to be approved by the curriculum committee of the undergraduate division, and then by the full faculty of that division.

Blacks Halt Protests

A B.S.A. spokesman said demonstrations would be suspended until the faculty votes on the proposal. The B.S.A. will hold a meeting tomorrow to work on the matter.

Weil thinks these campus explosions can be harnessed and "will reach a peak and decline this year if college administrators take a firm stand."

If the administrators don't do this, he fears that "radical, military groups such as the New Left may be counteracted by the formation of a New Right that will create more white racism than we have ever known."

"Students have justifiable grievances, and sometimes we take them too lightly," Weil said in a speech Wednesday at the Sherman House during the 64th anniversary meeting of the Rotary Club of Chicago. "We must find out what it is they want and what we can do about it.

"But we can't permit students to disrupt the very education that might be able to solve the problems that brought on the protests, such as war and racism."

Promises Harsh Discipline

Weil said, "If I have one job to do, it is to provide freedom to learn for those who want to learn, and freedom to teach for those who want to teach. I will use whatever discipline is needed—whether from the university or thru civil and criminal charges—to inforce this freedom.

"It is our responsibility to see to it that we use the funds given to us by taxpayers or from tuitions for the purpose for which the money was given to us."

Weil said, "There is a place for civil disobedience to call attention to wrongs by those who are willing to pay the price. There is a place for a hunger strike by a Ghandi, who was willing to die, or for demonstrations by a Martin Luther King, who was willing to go to jail.

"But these students break a law and then scream, 'Amnesty.'"

95

Part III.

Portals to Change

**"A university should be a
place of light, of liberty,
and of learning."**

*Benjamin Disraeli,
British statesman, 1804-1881*

8

The '70s – The New Educational Landscape

The greatest boom in the history of American higher education occurred during the '60s and the first half of the '70s. Not only was enrollment expanding but higher education was at or near the top of the list of priorities for public policy as well as institutionalized philanthropy. Leadership was provided by the Kennedy and Johnson administrations as well as by the Ford Foundation, the Carnegie Commission on Higher Education, Lilly Endowment, the Danforth foundation and others. Faculty morale was high due to expanding enrollments and research funds. Construction of educational facilities was visible across the country. It was commonly believed that private universities could not expand fast enough to meet the educational needs of the country, particularly in the urban areas where new population groups were looking to education for upward mobility opportunities.

Although it probably would have been impossible to stem the pressure for expanded public higher education, it was during this period that the opportunity was missed for introducing a national higher education voucher plan. Had such a plan been introduced, as proposed by many, including Milton Friedman and John Silber, the result would have been an improved allocation of educational resources and greater freedom of choice. Political reality, however, advocates grand schemes of public sector expansion, making empire building by public universities a foregone conclusion.

Although there is great merit in a balanced dual system of public and private higher education, it is unfortunate that the private sector has declined relatively throughout the post World War II period.

In the early '70s Roosevelt University viewed itself as a private university in the public interest and expanded its facilities substantially in order to meet the growing needs of a metropolitan area with a large minority population and first generation college goers. However, planning in an environment of great uncertainty about future competition was extremely difficult. Although the basic mission of the institution was never in doubt, serious questions arose regarding the niche we would fill as a result of a constantly expanding public sector under the "Master Plans" for higher education in Illinois.

That the University of Illinois in Chicago (UIC) had initially planned an exclusively undergraduate daytime program, exemplifies the problem. Promises were made to the private sector that UIC would not offer evening or graduate programs, nor would it use state resources to build dormitories. In hindsight I realized how naive many of us were to believe that these promises could be kept in the face of public pressures for expanded heavily subsidized higher education.

Much has been written about institutional cooperation, the success of which has been greatly exaggerated. Such cooperation only works if it is in the interest of all the institutions involved. This is particularly true with regard to highly esoteric and specialized subject matter. For example, one institution might teach Japanese and a neighboring university Chinese. During the '70s, Roosevelt tried a cooperative business education venture with Northeastern State University, an institution not initially authorized for a professional business curriculum. Northeastern's President Jerome Sachs proposed therefore that students interested in business subjects take them at Roosevelt with the state paying the differential between the state tuition and our instructional cost. This made eminently good sense and could have saved the state a substantial amount of money. Problems arose almost immediately. Predictably, Roosevelt University students resented paying a higher tuition for the same instruction as the state students. Moreover, after a few semesters, the data regarding the number of students enrolled in our program became the rationale for Northeastern's request for its own business curriculum.

I feel strongly that cooperation with the public sector in basic programs will not work as long as huge tuition differentials exist. This issue is made more complicated by the fact that the public has never understood or does not wish to understand the difference between cost and price. Obtaining exact cost data for the public sector is difficult, but an accounting study would undoubtedly show that the cost of educating a student at Roosevelt University is no greater than the cost at a comparable public institution. Yet the price differential has always been substantial. As a result the private sector has increasingly lost middle-class students to the public institutions where a subsidy equivalent to a substantial scholarship is granted to students regardless of need or ability.

In the middle '70s, this public policy brought about major changes in the composition of the Roosevelt student body. Whereas, during the University's first twenty-five years, it had served a significant number of middle-class Jewish students, this particular constituency declined sharply as a result of public institution expansion. In the early years we also served more full-time than part-time students and daytime enrollments were greater than evening enrollments. This situation was reversed as we approached the end of the decade. Moreover, the expansion of community colleges in the suburban areas as well as in the city forced Roosevelt increasingly into upper division and graduate curricula with concomitant higher costs.

It is often said that planning should be pro-active rather than reactive. However, with our basic mission and urban orientation, there was no alternative but to seek students who were inade-quately served by the public sector. As a result, Roosevelt became increasingly a transfer institution serving primarily part-time, upper division graduate and foreign students. Moreover, an increasingly large proportion of our student body came from lower income, inner city minority groups. It became imperative, therefore, that we find ways to attract a significant proportion of academically qualified students. Three markets were identified as ways of accomplishing our objective: adult students receiving tuition reimbursement, suburban students via the establishment of extension centers and out of town recruiting. The latter would require building a dormitory.

A discussion of public policy issues affecting private higher education in Illinois is not complete without praising an unusual study authorized by the General Assembly of the State of Illinois to deal with the future of private higher education. The results of this study, known as the McConnell Commission Report and entitled *Strengthening Private Higher Education in Illinois* were published in March 1969. Its recommendations, which included major expansion in the Illinois State Scholarship Program and the establishment of a Financial Assistance Act with significant funding based on enrollment of Illinois students, were never fully implemented. Nevertheless, nonpublic higher education would have shrunk to insignificance if it had not been for its partial implementation. During the 1980s I frequently suggested updating this report by another outside group of educators, a suggestion consistently ignored although supported by my independent education colleagues. The Board of Higher Education staff was apparently protecting its "turf" and its public higher education constituency.

Leadership for Change

Although a series of five-year plans were regularly prepared at Roosevelt, implementing them in the rapidly changing higher educational landscape required leadership support at the Board level. It was most unfortunate, therefore, that Lyle Spencer died unexpectedly and at an early age in the summer of 1968.

Lyle Spencer had been a complex person of unusual ability. His father had been an academic with administrative experience at the University of Washington and at Syracuse University. Spencer had planned an academic career for himself and was in a doctoral program in sociology at the University of Chicago during the Depression years. After Spencer completed his education, he founded, jointly with Robert Burns, a Ph.D. candidate in economics, Science Research Associates, initially a publisher of occupational guidance literature. When the United States entered World War II, Lyle Spencer served in the U.S. Air Force and worked jointly with Dr. Karl Menninger on programs to test potential pilots for their ability to withstand battle strain. As a result, Spencer's interest in testing converted Science Research Associates into a testing organization, a venture which became extremely successful. Spencer succeeded in combining business acumen with his scholarly pursuits. In fact, he considered Roosevelt University as a sort of research project. He was firmly convinced that the solution to interracial conflict lay in the provision for urban upward mobility education and that this was the way to overcome destructive racial conflict. Shortly before his death, Science Research Associates was sold to IBM and Lyle Spencer emerged as one of the wealthiest men in Chicago.

Lyle Spencer was no "bleeding heart," but a tough-minded pragmatist who wanted Roosevelt University to be a demonstration project in the area of urban education. During the last years of his life, he became a major financial contributor to the institution. Even more important, however, than his financial support was the fact that his Board leadership contributed significantly towards providing acceptance and recognition for Roosevelt by Chicago's business community. Indeed, on the occasion of the University's anniversary, the *Chicago Tribune* wrote an editorial entitled "From a Maverick to a Leader in Twenty-Five Years."

Lyle Spencer died near the end of July 1968, having recently been diagnosed with cancer of the pancreas. The progress of the disease was very rapid and he died a few weeks later. Memorial services were held at University of Chicago's Rockefeller Chapel. Eulogies were read by Ralph Tyler; T. Vincent Learson, Chief Executive Officer of IBM; and myself. He was buried in his hometown of Appleton, Wisconsin.

At the time of his death Spencer was a member of the Board of Lawrence University, the Menninger Foundation, and the University of Chicago, in addition to being Board Chairman at Roosevelt University. In view of these involvements and his substantial wealth, it was a great disappointment that none of these institutions was remembered in his will. The bulk of his wealth established the Spencer Foundation, which recognized Roosevelt in its early history through a one-time grant of $250,000. The Foundation has since pursued scholarly objectives, but without the pragmatic public policy concerns that always seemed uppermost in Lyle Spencer's mind during his lifetime.

On the other hand, Spencer's devotion to Roosevelt was exemplified by a deathbed gift at Passavant Hospital of $100,000. My friendship with Lyle and our shared objectives for Roosevelt led to my appointment as president. I owe him a great debt of gratitude for his all too short leadership role at the University.

Possibly the most important task of a private university president is to secure the best possible Board leadership. Although a Board Chairman is elected by the Board, the president of the institution normally plays a key role in convincing a trustee to take on the chairmanship, a position requiring time and dedication. The ideal chairman should also be in a position to make a substantial personal gift in support of the institution and should be able in this way to secure matching gifts from other Board members. I felt very fortunate that I could convince Jerome Stone, a long-time Board member and CEO of Stone Container Corporation, to take on the chairmanship after Spencer's death. My success in the presidency was due to a large extent to Stone's support for the institution. If Stone had not been led by circumstances into an entrepreneurial career, he undoubtedly would have reached the top in any of a number of professions. In him I found a man of intellectual acumen, an articulate advocate and above all a goal-oriented executive who, whenever the chips were down, would come to the rescue. His prior fundraising experience helped immensely in moving the University forward through the '70s and early '80s. In his fifteen years as chairman, Stone helped us to succeed with major development campaigns: "Up to Excellence," "Fulfilling the Promise," and "Over the Threshold to Greatness."

In my work with Lyle Spencer we succeeded in establishing the fiscal integrity of the institution and to offset Roosevelt

University's negative image in the business community. During Jerome Stone's chairmanship, and with the assistance of a superb vice president for development, Wendell Arnold, we changed the business community's "neutrality" with regard to Roosevelt into expanding and meaningful moral and financial support.

Construction To Meet New Needs

It became clear in the '60s that if Roosevelt was going to compete for students and faculty in the expanding '60s and early '70s markets, and in the increasingly competitive environment of the '80s, it would have to improve its facilities on the main campus.

Being the owners of a magnificent landmark building is not an unmitigated blessing. Although the Auditorium Building has turned out to be quite suitable for an educational institution, it required major renovation. Additional space also had to be found for the library and faculty offices as well as for student union facilities and housing.

During the '70s the University received several major gifts in support of expansion. One of the first of these was from the Crown family for the construction of the Herman Crown Center, a seventeen-story student union and residence hall for 350 students. A federal construction loan, plus the Crown money, enabled us for the first time to provide reasonably adequate facilities for student activities and dining. Although the Board of Trustees always understood that we would remain primarily a commuter institution, it was felt that a dormitory would add a new and important dimension in building "community." Early opinion surveys of students indicated that a very large number of students would wish to live in the facility immediately adjacent to the University on Wabash Avenue. To be able to go from a dormitory to a classroom without having to go outside during Chicago's winters seemed particularly appealing.

In hindsight I must concede that we were overly optimistic about dormitory occupancy and that surveys of students' hypothetical opinions are of very questionable value. Students have a short time horizon and those who answer a survey are not likely to be around when a construction project is completed. Moreover, students do not always have a clear view of their financial situation.

Roosevelt's administration wasted a great deal of time setting up priority schemes for housing allocation. This included a bitter confrontation with Joseph Creanza, Dean of Chicago Musical College, who believed that he could fill the dormitory with music students. As it turned out, only a small number moved in. Although the University needed the student union desperately and the dormitory provided opportunities for housing foreign and out-of-town students, we have never been able to get full occupancy through Roosevelt University students alone and have relied on students from neighboring institutions to make Crown Center financially viable.

It is worth recounting an incident that occurred at the Crown Center opening to illustrate the personal interest Richard J. Daley took in the city's development. The Crown Center was scheduled to open on a Sunday with a substantial number of students moving in with their belongings. On the preceding Friday evening, after most of us had gone home, a Fire Department captain informed our student union director that the building could not be opened because construction was continuing in the basement. The director informed me of this situation and that he was of the opinion that the captain may have been subtly asking for a "gift." We agreed that such a gift was out of the question for the University. When I suggested that he contact the fire commissioner, the director said he had done so, but the commissioner was on vacation and unreachable.

We could only appeal to the Mayor. I had no idea whether or where I could reach Mr. Daley. I called City Hall, which was closed for the day, and indicated to the policeman-guard my urgent need to reach the Mayor. He told me that the Mayor would be at the 11th Ward Democratic Committee Meeting that evening. I left word there, requesting an urgent conversation but doubting that I would get a response.

To my amazement the Mayor called a half hour later. I told

him that not opening the dormitory would be a disaster for the University, especially in view of the arrival of out-of-town students with no alternative housing available. he called me back in an hour, saying "I called the fire people and they were giving me a hard time because they said it would not be safe to open the dormitory. I told them that the good doctor said it was safe and if it is not safe, you are the fire people and it is your job to make it safe." I trembled. He continued, "I told them that I wanted the place patrolled by the fire department until it was safe and that should take care of your problem. I am also giving you my private home number and you can call me at any hour of the day or night if you need help." I thanked him profusely.

The Mayor's action, undoubtedly paralleled in similar situations, indicates not only his acute political sense but also a measure of his "hands on" administration of the city and its institutions. His actions were the very opposite of what one expects from bureaucracies.

The Heller Gift

In 1970 we received what at that time was the largest contribution in the history of the University in the form of a $2 million gift from the Walter E. Heller Foundation, whose president, Alyce DeCosta, became a member of our Board of Trustees and has remained a wonderful and supportive friend of the University. This gift, in addition to support under the Higher Education Facilities Act, enabled the University to undertake the construction of a ten-story classroom, laboratory, and library facility in what had been a light and air court in the center of the Auditorium Building.

Because of modern air-conditioning and lighting, it was possible to bridge the court area and to construct the ten-story facility from floors 2 to 11. This construction solved a critical problem involving library space. The University library had been located on the 10th and 11th floors and had not only inadequate space but also structural problems related to the heavy weight of books. The new construction included essential structural chang-es that improved the weight bearing ability of the space and provided air-conditioning for a large proportion of the old building, remodeled classrooms and completely rehabilitated the 8th floor tower on top of the building. Sullivan and Adler had designed this tower primarily for the purpose of housing huge water tanks which provided the hydraulic power source necessary to operate the original elevators and lifts in the Auditorium Theatre. These tanks were no longer needed after the installation of electric elevators and the Heller construction included the complete gutting of the inside of the tower, the installation of an elevator and the construction of modern air-conditioned offices in this new facility. Since my retirement in 1988, I have had the pleasure of occupying office space in the tower which was once part of the suite of offices of the Sullivan and Adler architectural firm and was once the highest point in Chicago, with an observation deck housing a weather bureau facility.

In recognition of the Heller Foundation gift, we named our business school the Walter E. Heller College of Business Administration and established the Walter E. Heller Lecture Series in International Business and Finance. This lecture series has brought to Chicago some of the most outstanding government and business leaders of the world, including Margaret Thatcher and Helmut Schmidt, and has been of tremendous help in establishing Roosevelt as a center for the discussion of public issues.

Adaptation to Demographic Change

With the dedication of the Herman Crown Center in 1971 and the Walter E. Heller Center in 1974, the major physical changes on our downtown campus were essentially completed. Alyce DeCosta's magnificent gift provided us with 30,000 square feet of entirely new space and 52,000 square feet of modernized, air-conditioned facilities.

In addition to the major Crown and Heller projects, mention must also be made of a $100,000 gift from the late Edgar Kaufman, a professor of architecture at Columbia University, for the restoration of the Michigan Avenue lobby. Two academically significant construction projects were the conversion of the Sinha

Lecture Hall into the O'Malley Workshop Theatre and the construction of the Fagen Art History Hall on the ninth floor. Roosevelt University's physical facilities by the mid-'70s were in excellent shape and located in what we proudly called the Cultures Crescent of Chicago, an appellation justified by Roosevelt's being surrounded by Orchestra Hall, the Art Institute, the Field Museum of Natural History, the Shedd Aquarium, and the Adler Planetarium. One could hardly find another campus so richly endowed with supportive resources for education.

Needless to say, physical facilities do not create quality education. Our rather standard curriculum had to be changed to meet new demographic needs and the competitive environment resulting from public policy. Although enrollment continued to rise to over a one-time high of 7,700 students in 1976, this statistic conceals more than it reveals. For an institution with so many part-time students, head count enrollment can be deceptive. Beginning in the mid-'70s, full-time equivalent enrollments started to decline and have remained below the 5,000 student level. This decline resulted from the expansion in the State system and was offset by our new thrusts in adult and suburban enrollment consisting to a great degree of part-time students.

A successful urban university must maintain, without quotas of any kind, a good mix of students by race, gender, income level, and age. Only in this way can the University be the city in microcosm and, in my judgment, provide an optimum educational environment. Such an environment cannot be brought about by fiat but can result from curriculum adjustments and by location and method of knowledge delivery. Four concepts went into our planning: external degree programs, cooperative education, nontraditional degree programs for adults, and urban centers to provide easier access to education.

Our efforts in the area of cooperative education, even with grant support, unfortunately failed. The reason cooperative education pioneered so successfully at Northeastern University in Boston and did not work at Roosevelt is because a large proportion of both our full-time and part-time students had already found jobs within the community, jobs which were more suited to their needs and better compensated than those that could be negotiated through our "Co-op" education office. Moreover, the students most interested in our cooperative education program were foreign students who were difficult to place. And employers were too frequently using the cooperative education device to meet their own seasonal needs without due regard for the program's educational objectives. After approximately three years of experimentation, the program was dropped.

Under a substantial 1977 grant of $250,000 from the Lilly Foundation, headed at that time by Dr. James Holderman, who had previously served as Executive Director of the Board of Higher Education of the State of Illinois, an external degree program was launched. The purpose of this knowledge delivery system was to service the isolated learner as well as the individual who had periodically to drop out of the regular curriculum for reasons of work schedule, illness, child rearing, etc. It was not meant to be simply another correspondence study program. It was hoped that ordinary correspondence would be supplemented with the exchange of audiotapes by the teacher and learner, the use of telephone communication and other technologies then on the drawing boards, such as facsimile transmission and computer networking. The concept has never fulfilled its promise, although I remain convinced that such programs are needed in our society. We still have an embryonic external degree system in existence, but it has been difficult to enlist faculty members to work in this mode without much greater compensation than could be afforded under existing tuition rates. Resistance to new technologies tends to persist for long periods of time.

One of the most successful innovations born of the necessity for building enrollments was the establishment of the Bachelor of General Studies program in the late '60s. The concept was path-breaking and controversial. Although copied by many institutions, the program was unique when introduced at Roosevelt by Professor Lucy Ann Marx and to a greater extent inspired by the teaching and writings of Professor Cyril Houle. It was based on the recognition that a time-shortened and flexible degree program would be appropriate for people over twenty-five with highly diverse educational backgrounds. A student's knowledge was assessed through the use of the College Level Examination Program (CLEP tests) developed by the Educational Testing Service of Princeton, New Jersey. The CLEP tests identified gaps in the student's general education so that educational requirements could be tailored to meet a student's needs. It was further determined that education should not follow traditional departmental lines but should draw on courses from many departments in order to meet the needs for broad, functional areas ranging from business to human services, etc. All students in the program were involved in an introductory course or "pro-seminar" to provide for a common educational experience and to enable mature individuals to return to a learning mode after a long absence from the classroom.

For this program to be acceptable to the traditional faculty, we had to make certain that its student and faculty quality would, if anything, be greater than for the University at large. Thus, a superb faculty was recruited in the 1970 academic year. The program became the major component of the new College of Continuing Education, which that year claimed 1,000 students over twenty-five years of age in our Bachelor of General Studies program. Dr. Marx, a woman of unusual ability and persuasive powers, succeeded in convincing a divided faculty senate that a separate faculty and administrative structure was a prerequisite for the success of this program, which continues to this day as one of Roosevelt's most attractive programs.

The other eminently successful effort which has attracted quality students and created diversity has been the University's efforts in the area of extension and branching. The original concept started in the mid-1950s when as a result of contacts made through Arthur Eckberg, our long-time Director of Career Planning and Placement, programs were established to make it possible for military personnel at the Fifth Army in Chicago, at Fort Sheridan and the naval command at Great Lakes to complete their degrees through a modular calendar and course offerings. At various times, in cooperation with Control Data Corporation this program was taken to Germany, Spain and Hawaii. After changes in manpower composition at Fort Sheridan and Great Lakes, programs were established at Glenview Naval Air Station, in Waukegan, and in Rolling Meadows.

With the decline of qualified military manpower in the Chicago area, the University needed a new and more permanent location in the north suburban area to serve not only the declining number of military personnel but more importantly the rapidly growing suburban civilian population. I asked Dr. Lawrence Silverman, our vice president for student services and a marketing expert, to explore possible new locations for a Roosevelt branch campus. As a result of his demographic studies, deliberation by the administration and contracts with School District 225 in Arlington Heights, the North School, a small school in that suburb was leased and became the main focus of our eminently successful expansion in the rapidly growing northwest suburban area. Sadly, Dr. Silverman died shortly after the opening of the Arlington heights campus. Fortunately, our vice president for development, Wendell Arnold, was a well-connected Arlington Heights resident who helped us overcome some of the initial political obstacles to expansion in that community—obstacles related primarily to the subtle suggestions by a fearful minority that we might bring bus loads of "undesirables" into the community. Nevertheless, community acceptance was and has continued to be most favorable.

Landmark Designation

The Auditorium Building is unquestionably one of the greatest accomplishments of 19th century American architecture. The issue of Chicago landmark designation in the 1970s became a major concern for Roosevelt University, not because of any disagreement regarding the worthiness of the building for designation, but because of a concern for potential restrictions on adaptive construction to meet educational needs. The building had been listed on the national register of historic places for many years and deservedly so. Not only is the Auditorium the creature of Sullivan and Adler, the founders of the Chicago School of Architecture with the young Frank Lloyd Wright as the cooperating draftsman, but it also was the site of two presidential nominating conventions. Benjamin Harrison was nominated by the Republican Party in the Auditorium Theatre in 1888 prior to its completion. Theodore Roosevelt was nominated in the same facility in 1912 by the Bull Moose Party.

The Chicago landmarks legislation provided among other things that no building permit could be issued with regard to a designated area until special approval had been granted, which could result in substantial delays. Some key Board members and I also felt that in a sense landmark designation constituted a taking of property without appropriate compensation.

Patrick O'Malley, an influential Board member, and I went to see Mayor Daley (I believe in 1975) to assure him that we would make every effort to preserve and restore the Auditorium Building without the potential legal entanglements involved in designation. The mayor assured us that if we did not want designation, it would not happen.

Less than a year later, however, two aldermen visited me in my office with a very persuasive argument in favor of designation. They told me that unless the Auditorium Building, one of the most significant structures in Chicago, was designated, the entire landmarks program was in jeopardy. Furthermore, they had the votes to push through the designation. They knew that the Mayor had promised to oppose the designation but they indicated how embarrassed the Mayor would be if he had to veto city council action on this matter.

Hearings were held on the landmarks issue on March 12, 1976, at which time I submitted testimony. The key paragraphs read:

"It is precisely because we wish to preserve and restore this facility that we must oppose designation. Without designation this University has been able to raise funds via the mortgage market, has been able to

113

adapt the building to educational use, and has adjusted flexibly and speedily to changing curricular conditions.

"With landmark designation Roosevelt University will find it difficult, even impossible, in the future to get the necessary and desirable mortgage financing for preservation and may be hampered through delays and additional costs in connection with necessary building alteration."

Testimony on behalf of Roosevelt University was also given by Philip Klutznick and Arthur Rubloff. While I was fully aware that we were not going to win, I was hoping for some compromise.

A satisfactory solution was found in negotiations between the Corporation Counsel of Chicago and our attorney, Robert Gorman. This provided for the designation of the facade of the building, the Sullivan Room, the Auditorium Theatre, the Oscar Fainman Lounge facing Michigan Avenue, Ganz Hall and the library reading room. Furthermore, there was an informal understanding that if we voluntarily agreed to this designation the Mayor would make every effort to make annual contributions towards the restoration of the building. This was an important victory because as I had frequently stated landmark designation by itself neither preserves nor restores; and that if as a matter of public policy we wanted to honor our great architectural monuments, funds must be made available to accomplish this objective. For several years under mayors Daley, Michael Bilandic and Harold Washington, we were able to get substantial amounts for preservation from moneys given to the City under the federal block programs.

The University in Public Service

Ever since its founding Roosevelt was dedicated to public service and to teaching for the urban area. Not only in its choice of literature but in its actions, the University considered itself not only in the city but of the city. It is not possible to list the many projects undertaken by Roosevelt in the interest of improving the quality of life in the Chicago community, the national and, in fact, the world.

Our endeavors included participation in the Teachers Corps Program, the Upward Bound Program for economically deprived students preparing for college careers, Peace Corps training to provide teachers for Sierra Leone, Cooperative Training Programs with the Illinois State Employment Service, a major mental health project in cooperation with the State of Illinois and the labor unions, etc.

Because much of our public service activity related to minority group problems, most of which related to matters involving the Chicago school system, we were determined to use our education faculty to spearhead research efforts and action programs in this area. Therefore, in 1972, our department of education was upgraded to college level. This change was controversial because of traditional objections from liberal arts faculties to colleges of education. The persuasiveness of Dr. Otto Wirth, our academic vice president, and the prospects of increased foundation and government support, convinced the faculty to approve this change. We also established a research and development center with a $250,000 start-up grant from the Spencer Foundation. Dr. Tom James, President of the Spencer Foundation at the time, and Dr. Bruno Bettelheim of the University of Chicago recommended that Dr. Robert Koff be the first dean of the College.

Since its establishment the College of Education has been a significant recipient of private and governmental grants to assist in every aspect of improving the urban learning environment. In the '70s there was evidence that Roosevelt University had been the largest private supplier of professional educators to the Chicago school system, a trend that undoubtedly continued.

9

The President
and University Management

During my years as president I developed a number of succinct and useful rules of behavior for university executives. There is nothing particularly original about these rules. They are adaptations of comments made by board chairmen and ordinary common sense and I have passed them over the years in the belief that they have had at least some impact on colleagues.

Rule 1: "Do not make promises you cannot keep."

It is tempting and satisfying to promise things that you believe in, but these feelings are more than offset by the disappointments that follow an unfulfilled promise. Such promises range from fundraising or enrollment goals, to salary levels, teaching load, promotions, or such small things as letters of appointments.

Rule 2: "Always have an alternative plan."

Strategic and tactical planning have become essential management tools, but I do not trust those who claim that most of their plans come to fruition. Sometimes alternative plans can be revealed; at other times they must be more or less confidential "fall back" positions. The key question is, "What will you do if. . . " For example, in the area of development, a fundraising goal is set. In order to avoid failure, it is desirable to refrain from setting a specific completion date. It is useful to have a category of giving, such as government support of a certain type, held in reserve for inclusion or exclusion in campaign goals. Similar alternative objectives can be set for enrollments, curricula, etc.

Rule 3: "Make things come out right."

I call this Lyle Spencer's commandment. It deals with the

"bottom line." It is a tough injunction but it sums up what most of administration is about. An occasional failure may be unavoidable, but with good judgment and a bit of luck a good administrator can make things come out right most of the time. Good intentions are not enough and failure in this category is serious.

Rule 4: "Remember that you get paid to take all the guff."

With the substitution of a more Saxon word for "guff," this originated with a former Roosevelt trustee, at the time a senior partner at Peat, Marwick and Mitchell. After a particularly difficult negotiating meeting in which I felt "left hanging," I explained my disappointment. He quoted the above rule, which has a good deal of merit. Often administrators, understandably, feel sorry for themselves, but compensation in the form of money, power or honor should be ample reward for managerial risk.

Rule 5: "Do not let your boss be caught by surprise."

This was another Spencer admonition. As a board chairman he was properly leaving the decision-making to the president. However, he relied on the president's judgment to keep him informed on matters such as student unrest, media issues, personnel changes which might later involve him. After once having excused a serious misstep by a dean as a rare lapse of judgment, Spencer said that lack of judgment is the most serious indictment against an administrator.

The Use of Consultants

While there are many situations in which consultants can be used advantageously, I am convinced that more money is wasted on such fees than in most areas of expenditure. Consultants are frequently called in when management is at a loss and has not even formulated a clear definition of what the consultant's task ought to be. Asking a consultant to make a study to tell you what you should do is a blatant abuse.

It is my experience that consulting projects should be narrowly defined and the objective clearly specified. The process of consultants writing their contracts and clients agreeing to them should be reversed. Less difficult is the development of consulting contracts for such matters as evaluation of insurance contracts, construction matters, accounting procedures, computer purchases, etc.

The most complicated consulting arrangements in university administration deal with the areas of planning, fundraising and public relations. For institutions with a good in-house professional staff, consultants are helpful in providing a periodic fresh outside evaluation of internal practices and in making what needs to be said more palatable because it comes from an outsider.

Without wishing to be unfair, I must say that at worst consultants say the obvious and parrot comments from the staff on the finest bond paper with lots of white space and leatherette cover. At their best, they provide new development ideas, articulate an institution's objectives to various publics, and create an improved climate for attaining objectives. Unfortunately, the client is often misled into believing that the consultant will raise money or improve public relations, each of which remains the client's responsibility.

The most difficult studies undertaken by development consultants are commonly known as feasibility studies, in which results can be critical but the findings are often questionable. It is essentially the consultant's task to determine through interviews the attitudes of Board members, major individual contributors and the business community towards the soliciting institutions. Unless these interviews are conducted by highly skilled individuals the results are often meaningless. Attitudinal studies have been undertaken by behavioral scientists with some success, but my experience does not support the belief that fundraising consultants employ associates with appropriate training or skill.

Raising Funds

One of my tasks as president was to assess how much could be raised in our various campaigns. Invariably each campaign was based on an inventory of academic needs which commonly exceeded by far the amount that, according to our feasibility assessment, could be raised. A consensus had to be reached between the president's recommendation and key players in the Board leadership regarding campaign goals. During my presidency the key fundraiser was Jerome Stone, both before he assumed the chairmanship and during his long tenure as chairman of the Board. At various stages of the University's history, Max Robert Schrayer, a vice chairman of the Board, and Dr. Milton Ratner, a former trustee, also played leading roles in our fundraising efforts.

In Roosevelt's early history, fundraising consisted primarily of large numbers of dedicated workers going out to solicit small amounts of money from all their friends, relatives and commercial suppliers of services. These endeavors during the Sparling years were primarily the result of Wells Burnette's efforts, assisted by Max Schrayer and others. I remember frequent report meetings where little old ladies proudly displayed several checks ranging from $25 to $100. These efforts would culminate in an annual dinner, at which results would be announced and a speaker would boost morale. The dinner provided a deadline date and was also used as a vehicle for raising additional funds. As discussed in earlier chapters, corporate support in those early years was relatively modest.

During the '60s, Wendell Arnold and I realized that for various reasons our "army" of fundraising supporters from the early years had shrunk significantly. Much discussion occurred at the Board level about whether a large new group, primarily alumni, should be recruited to continue the original fundraising format. Schrayer was a major advocate of this type of fundraising organization, patterned largely on techniques used by the Jewish United Fund, of which he had been fund campaign general chairman. He was probably one of the best fundraisers in Chicago and was also a good team player. We convinced him that in the '60s and early '70s our alumni had not yet attained the stature to successfully solicit funds from others. We therefore changed our emphasis on corporate, foundation and major individual gifts. In hindsight I wish we could have used both approaches, but given the budgetary operating restraints of the Development Office this would have been impossible.

When I took over the presidency, I was a fundraising novice and somewhat intimidated, but as time went on I adapted well to that part of my responsibility. A few anecdotes remain fresh in my memory. I had hardly been in office more than a few months when I was told that an outdoor advertising firm, which had a huge sign on North Michigan Avenue, with an electronic message below it, wanted to salute my new presidency. I did not know that the commercial above the salute was for Cutty Sark scotch. Our Board Chairman, Harland Allen, vehemently opposed alcohol and tobacco consumption, and called to reprimand me the first morning this salute appeared. I don't know whether his distress or mine was greater.

An even more serious mishap occurred a few months later when our alumni office director put a solicitation letter to alumni on my desk for my signature. I read it and complimented him on an excellent piece of work. A few days later Lyle Spencer called to tell me that President Beadle's office at the University of Chicago had telephoned to say that my letter to Roosevelt alumni was almost a verbatim copy of a letter Beadle had used. The alumni director resigned his position shortly thereafter.

Later, but still in my early years, I was eager to attract the attention of executive officers of national corporations. Usually I ended up seeing executives well below the CEO level, so I was quite amazed when the development office arranged an appointment for me with J.C. (Cash) Penney, founder of the major department store chain. Mr. Penney was in his nineties. I remember going to the Penney Building on the Avenue of the Americas for the meeting, armed with research about his interest in the Boy Scouts and Rotary International—organizations that I was also actively involved in both as a vice president of Rotary Club No. One and as a scout committee chairman. With great anticipation I took the elevator to the top floor and was greeted with what seemed unusual joy by Mr. Penney's receptionist. It seemed that Mr. Penney did not have many visitors. I was ushered into his presence almost immediately and began my presentation. I have always had a strong voice and am not accustomed to having listeners fall asleep. Nevertheless, Mr. Penney closed his eyes and only through repeated up and down modulation of my voice did I awaken him, at which time he told me about the hard times he was having. I decided that I had better take my leave before he dozed off again. I then knew why it was so easy to get this appointment.

At another point, Jerome Stone and Otto Geppert accompanied me to a meeting with a senior officer of the First National Bank of Chicago in order to solicit the bank's support for our "Up to Excellence" campaign. The gentleman had anticipated our visit and had prepared in advance an insultingly modest check. Our two Board members were so shocked by this that they politely refused to accept the check, said goodbye to our host and left me standing outside the door while each one rushed off to express his dismay to the vice president handling their respective accounts. Happily a much larger check arrived in the mail a week later. Moreover, the bank became one of Roosevelt's best corporate friends in subsequent years.

I will also never forget an incident that occurred when Stone and I met with Arthur Rubloff, a tall, lanky gentleman, who was wearing dark glasses and leaned across the conference table saying to Stone, "Jerry, I want you to know I am a wealthy, a very wealthy man but I simply do not have any cash to give away. In fact, if I had to raise cash right now, I would have to sell some of my wife's jewelry." With a smile on his face, Stone responded, "Which one of her pieces would you like to turn over to the University?" Although the legendary Rubloff made relatively small contributions in his lifetime, he left us a bequest in excess of $3 million. As it turned out the liquidation of his estate is taking years because of the illiquid nature of his investments.

It was my practice whenever possible to visit major contributors, corporate or individual, together with a trustee. If a trustee was not available, our vice president for development would accompany me. This was particularly true in my frequent visits to

New York, Minneapolis, Pittsburgh and the West Coast. One major lesson that Arnold and I learned early on was not to lose control over a fundraising contact by simply turning over the name of an individual or a corporation to a trustee. We did not want some of our well meaning friends to use solicitation letters or phone calls in lieu of personal visits, which, although more time consuming than writing a letter or making a phone call, usually resulted in larger gifts.

Finally, in memory of my wonderful friend, the late Max Robert Schrayer, allow me to include his favorite fundraising maxims.

First, people give to people more than to causes. There are certainly more good causes than can be supported by even the wealthiest of individuals. Therefore, the cause with the most effective spokesperson will get the funding. Second, ninety percent of the funds in a campaign come from ten percent of the contributors—a reliable yardstick for measuring fundraising potential. And third, only those who have themselves given significantly can successfully solicit others. Clearly, there is a pecking order, which is why it is extremely difficult to accept small gifts from individuals or companies that have given larger amounts to comparable institutions.

Presidential Survival

Because of my long tenure in office, I am frequently asked what it takes to survive successfully as president of a university. It seems to me that the chief executive officer of an academic institution faces greater obstacles than his or her counterpart in the corporate world. The main objective of a corporate CEO is to maximize profits. In the academic world the objective is to attain optimum enrollment, to contribute maximally to teaching, research and public service and to accomplish these objectives without significant fiscal deficits. Moreover, the university president must strive constantly to obtain consensus among several constituencies, including the Board, the administration, the faculty and the student body.

Success in university presidency depends on the establishment of credibility in terms of fiscal management with the Board and in terms of honesty and openness with the faculty. Between the president and top administrators mutual trust and loyalty are a priority. Students relate to excellence in instruction and minimization of excessive bureaucracy, especially in student services.

Possibly the most important skill is the ability to identify correctly the informal leaders who are not necessarily department chairmen or elected officers of the faculty senate. It is, in fact, crucial to have a "modus vivendi" with these leaders—not necessarily complete agreement on issues but a compatibility that makes cooperation possible even where there is an honest difference of opinion.

The university president cannot function effectively without the loyalty of the chief administrative officers. Disagreement and dissent prior to presidential decision-making should be encouraged, but once a decision has been made, loyalty is essential. During my years at Roosevelt, I faced only a few occasions where deans were unsupportive of policies agreed upon by myself and the majority of administrators. But this is inevitable since some deans consider their college their fiefdom.

Presidents normally face periodic crises, so one needs a strong psyche. It is impossible to be totally unemotional and it is only human to become upset at times. A president should never be overly joyful, angry or indecisive. Indeed, if properly controlled, such emotions can be administrative assets.

An administrator needs a balance in his or her life. I believe in the energetic pursuit of one's goals and have never shied away from a strenuous work schedule. However, becoming a workaholic who excludes family and recreation is an error. Travel, playing bridge with friends and hiking in the mountains have sustained my wife and me in times of great stress.

Presidential Freedom

Clearly, a president's freedom is circumscribed not so much by law or contract as by "custom and usage." Presidential lifestyle and political involvement are controversial issues. The presidents of small colleges, particularly parochial ones located in small communities, live in a goldfish bowl subject to innumerable stated and unstated restrictions. They live in the traditional "President's House," the official place for university entertaining. As Mrs. George Beadle explained to the wives of new presidents many years ago, when a university hires a president, they get two people for the price of one.

Fortunately, such a situation never prevailed at Roosevelt. Jim Sparling, the founding president, lived in his own suburban home. When Mr. Pitchell was appointed, the University sought a beautiful apartment in Hyde Park, about seven miles away from the campus. Nine years before I became acting president, we had moved to nearby Evanston and my wife, Leni, and my children did not wish to move back into the city. The University sold the Hyde Park apartment (unfortunately, at a considerable loss), and we received a modest housing allowance, thereby preserving our independence and having an opportunity to develop equity in real estate. I think that college presidents who must move out of the official residence when they retire and buy real estate with their life savings are in an unfortunate position.

When one lives a considerable distance from campus, there is also greater freedom in choosing friends and escaping the inbred social life characteristics of so many college towns. My family greatly valued this independence.

College presidents must, of course, involve themselves in community life although there is clearly a choice about how to do so. The nonsectarian nature of Roosevelt and its metropolitan setting contributed significantly to that freedom. Leni and I have always been involved with our synagogue and with a social agency, the Selfhelp Home for the Aged, founded by victims of Nazi persecution. I have served as vice president and president of this organization for over two decades, and our involvement has allowed us the opportunity to contribute significantly to a community which provided nurturing, stability and meaning to our own lives at a critical time. I have also devoted time to the Boy Scouts, Rotary, Landmarks Preservation Council of Illinois and the Executive Service Corps.

Although teaching has always been my first love, it was difficult to teach on any regular basis while serving as president. Often I team-taught an early morning course so the teaching did not seriously interrupt my day and the students were unaffected when I was out of town. Another drawback to an administrative career is the lack of time to conduct research in one's own field or even to keep current with the literature. Some exceptional people have combined administration and research, but I found it almost impossible.

The most interesting diversion during my presidency was consulting work for railroads and utilities in the field of public finance, particularly with regard to property tax equalization. I appeared as an expert witness in court cases all over the country. However, this had to be curtailed in the '70s because I had no time to update my expertise regarding new developments.

At many large universities corporate directorships become a major source of income and business contacts for presidents. Unfortunately, this has not been the case at Roosevelt—a pity because such board involvement can yield major fundraising benefits. However, I was privileged to serve for many years on the Carus Corporation board. I was particularly interested in their subsidiary, Open Court, which imaginatively pioneered humanistically oriented reading programs with an emphasis on phonetic methodology. Although their reading programs have been much imitated, their origins were conceptually unique and idealistically driven. A major reason for my appointment to that Board was that my background included a German humanistic Gymnasium education.

One of the most troublesome issues facing a university head is political involvement. Jim Sparling was often criticized for his close ties to labor unions, New Deal politics and world federalism. Such criticism seems unjustified, but it was my choice early in my career to avoid the complications of active political involvement. Although I supported certain nonpartisan issues, I never endorsed a political candidate or became actively involved in a campaign, thus avoiding possibly considerable controversy with students, faculty and board.

10

The Eighties – Preparing for Retirement

The late seventies and early eighties were extremely difficult years for private higher education in general and for Roosevelt University in particular. Double digit inflation, economic stagnation, enrollment declines, increased public sector competition and demographic changes combined to create serious problems.

Although Roosevelt salaries increased every year in the four to six percent range, inflation rates were above ten percent per annum, resulting in a decline of faculty and staff real income. Larger salary increases, however, were impossible because enrollment had been declining at our main downtown campus since its all-time high in 1976. Although head count enrollment declined gradually, tuition income was adversely affected by a shift from full-time to part-time students and from the traditional to the adult student population.

Over a period of many years Chicago experienced an exodus of the white population to the suburbs, a factor causing our downtown enrollment to become increasingly minority. As an institution with a strongly held philosophy of nondiscrimination and dedication to the inner city, Roosevelt was confronted with a number of challenges, including taking able but underprepared and culturally disadvantaged students and providing them with support services to prevent dropout and to prepare them for graduate education or for employment. This added to our operation costs, but we considered it a moral obligation.

Increased minority enrollment had both positive and negative consequences. It was a major argument for corporate support of the University. Our role contributed to racial harmony and provided corporate personnel at a time of affirmative action demands on the business community. However, it also made it more difficult to attract white ethnics who had traditionally been a main component of our student body before their exodus to the suburbs.

We were also confronted with the rapid expansion of the University of Illinois in Chicago. Many educators felt that this campus had been developed to provide much of the costly task of urban education, but escaped this responsibility by viewing itself as a developing research institution with a "quality" emphasis. Nevertheless, its proximity contributed to our enrollment decline. Fortunately, our own successful expansion in the suburbs helped subsidize the downtown campus, a situation that has continued into the nineties.

Although the faculty remained loyal and cooperative, morale clearly suffered from the economic adversity. Many faculty members, especially in the humanities, were discontent with their low salaries, a national phenomenon blamed on job opportunities drying up in these fields.

Adding to faculty anxiety in the early eighties were two administrative actions, taken reluctantly after faculty consultation and for the fiscal protection of the institution: the reduction in force (RIF) document of 1981 and a change in the date for salary increase announcement.

Until the eighties, faculty salaries, including annual increments, were committed in April for the following academic year before we had clear evidence of fall enrollment. Thus, an enrollment decline could force serious program cutbacks in order to meet contractual commitments regarding salary increases. To protect ourselves from such a situation, we initiated the practice of announcing salary increases after fall enrollment was complete.

In times as uncertain as the early eighties, it was reassuring to know that the budget committee, albeit in long and difficult sessions, would become intimately familiar with fiscal matters, providing credibility for the administration along with excellent advice and support. I felt keenly responsible for preserving Roosevelt's fiscal integrity, particularly knowing how dependent so many of our 500 employees were on their income. I had many sleepless nights in those years of declining enrollment, especially during fall registration in the late seventies and early eighties. I knew it was time to decide on retirement no later than age 67.

Fortunately, my private fears based on statistical data were only partly validated. Fundraising did not suffer from our changing priorities and enrollment in the suburbs increased beyond expectations. New curricula downtown—including paralegal studies, journalism and public relations, industrial engineering, computer science and telecommunications and hospitality management—helped substantially to offset declining enrollments.

The "Landmark of Quality" Campaign

The largest fundraising campaign of my administration was a $25 million drive which was successfully completed by the time I retired in the fall of 1988. The campaign had four major components: operating needs, new academic programs, physical plant needs and suburban development. Wendell Arnold and his successor, Robert Shepard, provided the executive staff support.

To support our institution we relied on publicly available data indicating the quality and societal significance of Roosevelt. A study by the National Academy of Sciences ranked 867 private non-Ph.D. granting colleges and universities according to the number of graduates who subsequently earned doctorates. In spite of its relatively short history, Roosevelt ranked in the top five percent.

A 1986 Educational Testing Service report singled out eleven predominantly white schools as "the most productive undergraduate institutions of black scientific talent." Roosevelt was one of the eleven, which included such prominent institutions as Stanford, University of Chicago, University of Michigan, Harvard and Brown among others.

"Black Issues in Higher Education," another study published in 1985, listed the 20 predominantly white institutions which granted baccalaureates to the largest number of blacks who eventually earned Ph.Ds from 1975 through 1980. Roosevelt ranked number 14 with 33 Ph.Ds.

The success of the fundraising campaign was based on tireless board participation and included the establishment of the Robin campus, the Logan Chair in History, and the Steinfeld Program in Hospitality Management. Two bequests towards the end of my tenure put the campaign "over the top": a $3 million bequest from former trustee Arthur Rubloff and another $3 million bequest from alumnus Marvin Moss. Both deserve a few comments about the hazards and opportunities in donor cultivation.

Arthur Rubloff can best be described as a legend in his own lifetime. No one was completely certain about his origins and many doubt the veracity of his autobiographical comments. He was proud of the fact that he had received almost no formal education. Supposedly his father was a prizefighter or wrestler. Arthur was born in Minnesota and came to Chicago as a young man. In his career as a real estate man he developed a reputation for a mixture of shrewdness, ruthlessness and generosity. He was easily offended and could bear a grudge for years. On several occasions he complained to me that he could never forgive Jim Sparling for having rented some small stores in the Roosevelt University building through another leading agent. Obviously, the amounts involved had to be insignificant in the context of the volume of his business. Nevertheless, he kept harping on this issue.

Even though Rubloff made consistent, relatively small gifts to us, we were never able to get a major contribution during his lifetime. In fact we were greatly distressed when he made $10 million pledges to the University of Chicago and to Northwestern University. I felt deeply hurt by the fact that these contributions were made to institutions which undoubtedly would not have considered him for Board membership.

Rubloff's potential for vindictiveness occurred during a luncheon for major alumni donors. He was very generous about lending his company's private dining room for special occasions. During such events he displayed his valuable paperweight collection, which eventually became a gift to the Art Institute of Chicago. He would also distribute to the invited guests token gifts, such as a Civil War vintage replica of General Ulysses S. Grant's shoehorn. On the occasion of our luncheon he spotted one of our alumni, who had been an employee of his in earlier years. Rubloff called me aside to tell me that he had a gift for everybody but none for this individual because "that s.o.b. left my firm and competed with me." I had to plead with him to avoid giving gifts to anyone under the circumstances. He agreed with some reluctance.

During his last years Arthur Rubloff, in my opinion, showed signs of loneliness. He would appear at meetings of the Committee of 100 of the Council on Foreign Relations and sit in a chair during the cocktail hour with no one to talk to. I tried to keep him company on such occasions. Rubloff had a great love for the city of Chicago and his bequests to the community were magnanimous indeed.

The Moss bequest is another fascinating illustration of the rewards that can come to an institution through long cultivation. Marvin Moss graduated from Roosevelt in the institution's early history. He worked for Music Corporation of America and eventually went on his own as a talent agent. The Development Office identified him early on as an individual who had made spontaneous gifts of three digits to the institution. As a result I visited him almost annually over a period of years whenever I went to Los Angeles. Invariably he invited me for lunch. In spite of my efforts to increase his giving to the four digit level, he rejected the request, saying "some day you will get more of my money." As he was a relatively young man, I was disappointed. During my last visit, Moss told Robert Shepard, our then vice president for development, and me that he was suffering from a terminal carcinoma. Soon after he died we were notified by the executor that we were the residual heirs of his will.

His will, which had been drawn up with the assistance of an entertainment lawyer, was most unusual. It provided for a black-tie dinner in his memory, at which wine from his own cellar was to be served, but no more than one bottle per invited guest to avoid making it into a wine-tasting party. He provided for a gift of his own condominium to a woman friend, provided that at the time of his death she and he had a loving relationship. He appointed a committee of three men to make this determination. His gift to Roosevelt directed the University to construct facilities to improve the social life he missed during his own student days there.

Unfortunately, the unusual nature of the will caused the trust department of his bank to drag out the probating of the document. We had to retain our own attorney in California to prevent what, in our judgment, were abuses in the will's administration. We were quite sensitive, however, knowing that as residual heirs all incurred expenses reduced the amount left to us.

The great variety of factors which motivate donors has always fascinated me. Other examples of major gifts received by Roosevelt during my presidency illustrate a variety of philanthropies. I have previously mentioned the Heller Foundation and Stone family gifts which we received during the early years of my presidency. Alyce DeCosta, who had been married to Walter Heller, made the first major foundation gift to Roosevelt University. The presence on our Board of Norman Mesirow, Gerald Gidwitz and Jerome Stone contributed significantly to her interest in our institution. I believe that Alyce DeCosta genuinely enjoyed the process of perpetuating the name of her late husband by contributing to significant causes. We prepared an elaborate presentation to her and she made her decision quickly and remained a true friend in subsequent years.

The naming of our college of continuing education in memory of Evelyn Stone, the first wife of Jerome Stone and the mother of his three children, was motivated not only by feelings of "noblesse oblige" for a long-time Board Chairman, but also by his deeply felt love for a wife who suffered for years from Alzheimer's disease. Stone's devotion to his wife during her long illness was exemplary. It also explains why he almost single-handedly created the Alzheimer Foundation, putting the fight against this dreadful disease high on the priority scale of public health issues.

Albert Robin, for whom we named our Arlington Heights campus, built his construction business during the great depression and throughout his career exhibited a desire to help the people and the community that had enabled him to accumulate wealth in one generation. He wanted to give back to the community, during his lifetime, some of the profits he had earned over the years. He sought my advice on setting up a scholarship foundation to assist graduates of Chicago schools in pursuing higher education objectives. With the assistance of our college of education, we helped him launch this generous effort. Al had always promised that at some point in the future he would do something specifically for Roosevelt. My wife Leni and I discussed our interest in the Arlington Heights expansion with Al and his wife Connie one evening at dinner. At a subsequent luncheon this major gift was finalized. The Robin Campus was able to become successful largely because of this investment by a generous donor.

The Manfred Steinfeld Program in Hospitality Management grew out of another fascinating Chicago biography. Manfred Steinfeld was a victim of Nazi persecution who came alone as a teenager to Chicago. Much of his family did not survive the Holocaust. After his military service, Manny studied at Roosevelt and in one of my classes in public finance he learned how to obtain a State of Illinois civil service position. (He performed the same functions that had been my responsibility a few years earlier.) After a short period he left this job to enter the furniture business and thus began a truly Horatio Alger journey toward attaining great wealth in the contract furniture industry. A major supplier of seating furniture for hotels and restaurants, Steinfeld responded with particular interest to our needs for a hospitality management curriculum. When we finalized his gift, his joy at giving the largest alumni gift to date was obvious. For me it was particularly meaningful to receive this gift from someone whose background was so similar to my own.

One of the last major gifts secured for Roosevelt came from Renee Logan, who had served on our Board for a relatively short time when I appealed to her to establish a professorship in our College of Arts and Sciences in memory of her late husband. A very gracious and cultured lady, with deep human concerns, she was most interested in the social sciences and eager to help. As a result, Roosevelt University now has a Seymour Logan Chair.

The Divestment Issue

During the 1983-84 academic year, Jerome Stone was succeeded as Board Chairman by Bart van Eck, a vice president of FMC Corporation and a soft-spoken, highly intelligent corporate executive. He was a conservative and a man of high integrity who held strong opinions unquestionably influenced, at least to some extent, by the FMC culture. During his administration, the issue of investment in South African companies became a major issue on American campuses. Roosevelt University's portfolio was minuscule by any measure and we owned no securities with major holdings in South Africa. Moreover, the companies whose stock we owned and who had some involvement in South Africa had all subscribed to the Sullivan principles. (Leon Sullivan, an important leader in the black community, had developed these principles to encourage racial integration in South Africa.)

Van Eck felt strongly that while we should in no way support South African apartheid policies, we would be violating our fiduciary responsibility if we did not put our fiscal needs ahead of socio-political considerations. Moreover, he believed that once we gave in to pressure on this issue, we would eventually face similar difficulties about stock holdings in companies involved in defense, pollution, etc. He and I both felt that foreign policy was a matter for Washington and that pressure should be legitimately applied to the government rather than to individual institutions. The Roosevelt Board voted overwhelmingly to maintain our investment decisions purely on fiduciary considerations.

I was, of course, concerned about repercussions in this matter. Fortunately, the politics of the eighties did not create the upheaval that might have occurred had we taken this position in the sixties, although the higher education community was, of course, very much divided on this issue.

Retirement Initiatives

In the early eighties, towards the end of Jerome Stone's chairmanship, I began to discuss my retirement. although I had no specific date in mind, I felt that it was in my interest as well as that of the University to consider a number of alternatives, including the possibility of returning to full-time teaching. Stone appointed a committee under the chairmanship of Max Robert Schrayer to work through all the retirement issues including financial arrangements under alternative assumptions. The Board of Trustees accepted the report, which was in every way satisfactory to me. I was reassured by the Board's frequently expressed desire to keep me in office as long as possible and filed away the report for several years.

My highest professional priority was to have the University in the best possible shape at the time of my retirement. This involved not only a great deal of fiscal planning, but also a degree of good luck. A balanced budget and no accumulated deficit were always my greatest wish throughout the middle eighties. I felt fortunate that we balanced our budget during every year in my final decade. With the help of three board chairmen, Jerome Stone, Bart van Eck and, beginning with the 1986-87 academic year, Alan Anixter, we were able to build up reserves for contingencies.

Bart van Eck's resignation as Board Chairman, which came as a surprise, resulted from a restructuring at FMC Corporation, wherein van Eck took early retirement and moved to California. His tenure in the chairmanship was short, but we had a close working relationship and his presence on our Board was extremely helpful in strengthening our ties to the corporate community.

It was necessary to persuade someone to take over the Board chairmanship before I could implement my retirement plans. This is not an easy task for the chairmanship is time-consuming and involves significant financial commitment. The Board Chairman had to be someone who understood the role of Roosevelt University, respected the higher education mission of a private institution and possessed the personal characteristics that would inspire confidence in the University's various publics. As I had done so frequently in critical moments, I called on Jerome Stone for assistance. We decided that he should try to convince Alan Anixter to take over the job. Anixter had both an academic and practical background and had excellent connections in the telecommunications industry. The Anixter choice was a fortunate one and he was most helpful during my two final years in the presidency. Although he most graciously asked me to defer my retirement, we agreed that a formal search for a successor should be initiated in 1987. Then I could retire in the fall of 1988 at age 67, after 23 years at the helm.

I recommended to the Board Chairman the composition of a search committee, which was carefully selected to represent the Board, alumni, student body, with appropriate representation by women, minorities and different segments of the academic community. We were most fortunate that our Board member David Ferguson, retired from U.S. Steel and an expert on public relations, was willing to accept the chairmanship, obviously a crucial one. Although I felt that Ferguson would handle this delicate assignment with distinction, he played his role to perfection with the greatest diplomatic skill. All constituencies cooperated and he built morale both on the committee and in the faculty. His regular reports to the senate with regard to the search allayed fears and uncertainties which could have arisen with a less able person.

The search committee's first task was to select a search consultant. After interviewing several firms, the committee retained the Presidential Search Consulting Service, at that time a subsidiary of the Association of Governing Boards. Dr. Ronald Stead served as our consultant.

Preparing for the Transition

Many universities suffer a collective trauma during a period of presidential transition. Except for a short-term presidency in

1964, Roosevelt had been served only by its founding president Edward J. Sparling from 1945 through 1963 and by myself from 1965 to 1988. The first transition, described in Chapter VI, had been extremely difficult and I was deeply concerned that this not occur again. I impressed on Ferguson the importance of avoiding a selection "mistake" and he certainly proceeded with great care, following, with the committee, the guidelines for presidential recruitment that were spelled out in ample literature on the subject.

During the search, Ferguson kept me informed of the progress and I had the opportunity to meet the "finalists." The entire process went remarkably well. My personal soul-searching regarding changes that should be made in the governance structure and personnel of the University prior to my departure was intense.

Unusual as substantial faculty representation on the Roosevelt University Board of Trustees may be, I felt that it was not crucial to make a change and, in fact, a reduction in faculty Board representation could have had serious morale consequences. I had also become convinced that faculty participation in budget-making constituted a strength for the institution, especially in periods of fiscal restraint. As discussed in Chapter V, I felt that the votes of confidence on administrators had an overwhelming negative impact. Clearly it would be difficult to find an outstanding educational leader as president with these institutionalized votes of confidence. Furthermore, if an educator was willing to accept the challenge but would have to change the system early in his or her administration, the new president would be confronted with a major internal upheaval. I suggested to Ferguson that he discuss this with Dr. Stead, who felt strongly that the University bylaws should be amended to remove the provision for triennial votes of confidence. Ferguson skillfully explained the need for change to the faculty senate and we succeeded in getting appropriate Board action without major conflict.

I also evaluated my administrative staff, fully aware of strengths and weaknesses in the top administration. I could have made some changes prior to my leaving, but decided, I believe correctly, that it would have been a mistake. A new president should make his or her own assignments and choose the team.

My successor was selected in the spring of 1988. The University was in excellent fiscal shape—the 1988-89 budget was in place with adequate reserve funds and with gift commitments that would assure a balanced budget.

Although my retirement arrangements, which had been agreed to several years earlier, gave me a choice of full-time or less than full-time teaching on prorated salary with tenure status, I did not take advantage of this generous offer. Instead, I decided to teach on a part-time basis during fall semesters, which would enable Leni and me to travel in January and February. In view of my 42 years of employment, at very low salaries in the early years, the Board provided me with a financial settlement to supplement my retirement pension income. I was also given office space and secretarial support as had been provided for Sparling.

For the first half of 1988 Leni and I went from one retirement party to the next. We were immensely pleased by the outpouring of appreciation from friends as well as academic antagonists. We were being honored by students, faculty, staff, alumni and the Board of Trustees. A major event was a reception in the foyer of the Auditorium Theatre for all constituencies on April 27, 1988. A huge ice sculpture was centered on the buffet table and students from Chicago Musical College provided beautiful music.

Throughout its history Roosevelt University has had a family feeling about it. There have been disputes, struggles for survival, happy occasions and disappointments, but there has always been an underlying spirit of community and a pulling together in periods of crisis. So many of us owed so much to this institution that provided opportunity in a democratic, nondiscriminatory environment. Leni and I developed an almost proprietary love for this place and will always support it as it develops and changes to meet new needs.

The highlight of my final months was a formal farewell party at the Ritz-Carlton Hotel on October 4, 1988, arranged by the

Board of Trustees with wide community participation. Several surprises awaited Leni and me on that occasion. The establishment of a professorship in my name was announced, Leni received a beautiful cameo as a gift, and both of us were given a trip to the Yukon and Alaska. The greatest surprise was a video presentation covering my 42 years at Roosevelt as a full-time faculty member and administrator. David Ferguson had made arrangements for a truly professional presentation narrated by Bill Kurtis of CBS and accompanied by Mozart's "Eine Kleine Nachtmusik." I was totally surprised and thrilled by this magnificent sendoff and most pleased by the presence of so many trustees, friends and associates. It was particularly satisfying to welcome two former university vice presidents who had moved on to presidencies of their own, Daniel Perlman of Suffolk University (now at Webster University) and Paul Olscamp of Bowling Green University. David Ferguson served as master of ceremonies and Jerome Stone, to whom I owe so much, spoke with his usual eloquence.

The greatest honor that the Board bestowed on me, however, was their recommendation to add me to the governing Board of Trustees. Because this offer could potentially create a problem for my successor, I made it eminently clear that I would accept only if he had no objection.

The Succession

As I am writing these reflections in 1991, almost three years after Dr. Theodore Gross took over the presidency, I am delighted to know that the University is in good hands. Dr. Gross has been more than gracious in his relationship with me and I have tried to the best of my ability to be helpful to him in his difficult and important assignment.

Dr. Gross was selected by the Board of Trustees based on his previous administrative experience. His considerable scholarly attainments and his ability to articulate the needs of urban education in partnership with the schools and the corporate community were major factors leading to his selection.

Very little has been written about the role of the president emeritus at colleges and universities. In the corporate community chief executive officers usually become chairmen of the executive committee and subsequently remain on their boards for a limited number of years. In some educational institutions presidents become chancellors with fundraising responsibilities but without operating authority. This type of shared authority can create serious problems for a new president because of divided loyalties that might result. However, if the incoming president and the president emeritus are reasonably compatible, it would be a mistake for the new president not to take advantage of the assistance that the former incumbent might voluntarily provide. Dr. Gross invited me early in his tenure to help him make contacts with important community leaders and I have been happy to do so.

A new administration inevitably will and should make changes in the way an institution is operated. Continuity is important but gradual change in administrative structure, in policies and in long-range planning is essential for institutional renewal. In my short period as a board member with emeritus status, I have tried to speak up only on rare occasions and in support of the policies of the new administration. I believe that such a role is helpful to a successor and constitutes responsible behavior. Just as the change from the founding administration of Jim Sparling constituted a major turning point in the history of the institution, so will Dr. Gross's stewardship provide opportunities for new and different approaches towards the objectives of improved higher education for a metropolitan area with a myriad of social problems.

At this point in my life I am grateful for so many things. Most important is the balance I have been able to maintain between professional responsibility, involvement in philanthropy and a happy family life. Part-time teaching, a continuing relationship to Roosevelt University and involvements with the Landmarks Preservation Council of Illinois, the Executive Service Corps and above all with the not-for-profit Selfhelp Home for the Aged keep me busy and useful to society. I am fortunate to have the part-time assistance of Mary Sonoda, who has the longest employment tenure of anyone at Roosevelt University. Miss Sonoda started to work for Jim Sparling in 1945, survived the difficult interregnum of 1964 and has been associated with me ever since.

It is my hope that Roosevelt University will grow and flourish as I watch from the sidelines. Its task will always be one of flexible adjustment to changing urban needs and a preservation of the founding values of equal educational opportunity for all members of society who can benefit from a quality education.

INDEX